I am a Hypocrite

Ibn Qayyim

Copyright

Introduction

And they ask you (O Muhammad) about the Ruh (the Spirit); Say: The Ruh (the Spirit): it is one of the things, the knowledge of which is only with my Lord. And of the knowledge, you (mankind) have been given only a little.

وَيَسْـَٔلُونَكَ عَنِ ٱلرُّوحِ ۖ قُلِ ٱلرُّوحُ مِنْ أَمْرِ رَبِّى وَمَآ أُوتِيتُم مِّنَ ٱلْعِلْمِ إِلَّا قَلِيلًا ﴿٨٥﴾

O People of the Scripture, do not commit excess in your religion or say about Allah except the truth. The Messiah, Jesus, the son of Mary, was but a messenger of Allah and His word which He directed to Mary and a soul [created at a command] from Him.

So believe in Allah and His prophets and messengers. And do not say, Three; desist-it is better for you. Indeed, Allah is but one God. Exalted is He above having a son. To Him belongs whatever is in the heavens and whatever is on the earth. And sufficient is Allah as Disposer of affairs.

يَٰٓأَهْلَ ٱلْكِتَٰبِ لَا تَغْلُوا۟ فِى دِينِكُمْ وَلَا تَقُولُوا۟ عَلَى ٱللَّهِ إِلَّا ٱلْحَقَّ إِنَّمَا ٱلْمَسِيحُ عِيسَى ٱبْنُ مَرْيَمَ رَسُولُ ٱللَّهِ وَكَلِمَتُهُۥٓ أَلْقَىٰهَآ إِلَىٰ مَرْيَمَ وَرُوحٌ مِّنْهُ فَـَٔامِنُوا۟ بِٱللَّهِ وَرُسُلِهِۦ وَلَا تَقُولُوا۟ ثَلَٰثَةٌ ٱنتَهُوا۟ خَيْرًا لَّكُمْ إِنَّمَا ٱللَّهُ إِلَٰهٌ وَٰحِدٌ سُبْحَٰنَهُۥٓ أَن يَكُونَ لَهُۥ وَلَدٌ لَّهُۥ مَا فِى ٱلسَّمَٰوَٰتِ وَمَا فِى ٱلْأَرْضِ وَكَفَىٰ بِٱللَّهِ وَكِيلًا ۝١٧١

Those Messengers! We preferred some to others; to some of them Allah spoke (directly); others He raised to degrees (of honor); and to Iesa (Jesus), the son of Maryam (Mary), We gave clear proofs and evidences, and supported him with Ruh-ul-Qudus [Jibrael (Gabriel)]. If Allah had willed, succeeding generations would not have fought against each other, after clear Verses of Allah had come to them, but they differed-some of them believed and others disbelieved. If Allah had willed, they would not have fought against one another, but Allah does what He likes

۞ تِلْكَ ٱلرُّسُلُ فَضَّلْنَا بَعْضَهُمْ عَلَىٰ بَعْضٍ ۘ مِّنْهُم مَّن كَلَّمَ ٱللَّهُ ۖ وَرَفَعَ بَعْضَهُمْ دَرَجَٰتٍ ۚ وَءَاتَيْنَا عِيسَى ٱبْنَ مَرْيَمَ ٱلْبَيِّنَٰتِ وَأَيَّدْنَٰهُ بِرُوحِ ٱلْقُدُسِ ۗ وَلَوْ شَآءَ ٱللَّهُ مَا ٱقْتَتَلَ ٱلَّذِينَ مِنۢ بَعْدِهِم مِّنۢ بَعْدِ مَا جَآءَتْهُمُ ٱلْبَيِّنَٰتُ وَلَٰكِنِ ٱخْتَلَفُوا۟ فَمِنْهُم مَّنْ ءَامَنَ وَمِنْهُم مَّن كَفَرَ ۚ وَلَوْ شَآءَ ٱللَّهُ مَا ٱقْتَتَلُوا۟ وَلَٰكِنَّ ٱللَّهَ يَفْعَلُ مَا يُرِيدُ ﴿٢٥٣﴾

Ibn Al-Qayyim Al-Jawziyya

His father was the director of a school called Al-Jawziyya which was located in the Damascus Wheat Market and for that reason he was called Ibn Al-Qayyim Al-Jawziyya.

He is not the same as Ibn Al-Qayyim Al-Jawzi who died in Baghdad in 597 A.H.

Ibn Al-Qayyim Al-Jawziyya was born into a scholarly and virtuous family in 691 A.H. / 1292A.D. At that time Damascus was a center of literature and thought. Many schools were located there and he studied and graduated under the protection, direction and sponsorship of his father.

He was particularly influenced by his Shaykh and teacher Ahmad b. Taymiyyah, and also by Ibn ash-Shirazi amongst others.

When he had reached maturity and had become a scholar of weight and reputation, he started to teach at Al-Jawziyya and had many students, including Ibn Kathir. He was looked to as a model in both youth and middle-age, by reason of the fact that he went out of his way to pass on to others the knowledge he had been given by those who came before him.

From his youth onwards he was constantly striving, tireless in his examination of everything around him, brilliant. Throughout his life, he remained an example of humility.

He was calm and convivial, constant in worship, getting right to the core of the deen (religion), a living example of the meaning of scrupulousness. He was courageous about stating the truth, no matter what the consequences.

After memorizing the Noble Quran, he set about memorizing hadith and then turned to poetry, studying language through the different periods of poetic development. Then he immersed himself in the field of Islamic culture, paying particular attention to legal judgment s. He collected books and extracted all that could be extracted from them. He took a long time over the books he wrote, taking great pains in his research and accuracy so that he would produce definitive, coherent works for people from which nothing had been left out.

For that reason people were hungry for his words and his books were widely read.

Imam Hafiz Ibn Kathir (14/234) said: He was constant in humbly entreating and calling upon Allah. He recited very well and had very fine manners. He did not harbor any envy or malice towards anyone, and he never sought to harm or find faults. I was one of those who most often kept company with him and was one of the most beloved of people to him. I do not know of anyone in the world in this time, who is better than him. His prayer used to be very lengthy, with very prolonged bowing and prostrations. Some colleagues would criticize him for this, yet he never retorted back, nor did he abandon this prayer. May Allah bestow His mercy upon him.

His Death

Imam Ibn Qayyim passed away at the age of sixty, on the 13th night of Rajah, 751H, may Allah shower His Mercy upon him.

Sifat Al-Munafiqin

All praise and thanks are due to Allah, we praise Him, ask His aid, and ask His forgiveness. We take refuge with Allah (SWT) from the evil of our souls and the evil of our deeds. Whoever Allah guides, none can ever misguide; and whoever Allah leaves to stray, none can ever guide. I bear witness that none has the right to be worshipped but Allah, and Prophet Muhammad (peace be upon him) is His servant and final Messenger.

يَٰٓأَيُّهَا ٱلَّذِينَ ءَامَنُوا۟ ٱتَّقُوا۟ ٱللَّهَ حَقَّ تُقَاتِهِۦ وَلَا تَمُوتُنَّ إِلَّا وَأَنتُم مُّسْلِمُونَ ﴿١٠٢﴾

O you who have believed, fear Allah as He should be feared and do not die except as Muslims [in submission to Him]. (3:102)

This is the Book (the Quran), whereof there is no doubt, a guidance to those who are Al-Muttaqun [the pious and righteous persons who fear Allah much (abstain from all kinds of sins and evil deeds which He has forbidden) and love Allah much (perform all kinds of good deeds which He has ordained)]. (2:2)

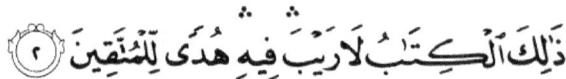

Like a rainstorm from the sky, wherein is darkness, thunder, and lightning. They thrust their fingers in their ears to keep out the stunning thunderclap for fear of death. But Allah ever encompasses the disbelievers (i.e. Allah will gather them all together). (2:19)

$$\text{أَوْ كَصَيِّبٍ مِنَ السَّمَاءِ فِيهِ ظُلُمَاتٌ وَرَعْدٌ وَبَرْقٌ يَجْعَلُونَ أَصَابِعَهُمْ فِي آذَانِهِم مِّنَ الصَّوَاعِقِ حَذَرَ الْمَوْتِ وَاللَّهُ مُحِيطٌ بِالْكَافِرِينَ ﴿١٩﴾}$$

And seek help in patience and As-Salat (the prayer) and truly it is extremely heavy and hard except for Al-Khashiun [i.e. the true believers in Allah - those who obey Allah with full submission, fear much from His Punishment, and believe in His Promise (Paradise, etc.) and in His Warnings (Hell, etc.)]. (2:45)

$$\text{وَاسْتَعِينُوا بِالصَّبْرِ وَالصَّلَاةِ وَإِنَّهَا لَكَبِيرَةٌ إِلَّا عَلَى الْخَاشِعِينَ ﴿٤٥﴾}$$

Fear your Lord, who created you from one soul and created from it its mate and dispersed from both of them many men and women. And fear Allah, through whom you ask one another, and the wombs. Indeed Allah is ever, over you, an Observer. (4:1)

$$\text{يَٰٓأَيُّهَا ٱلنَّاسُ ٱتَّقُوا۟ رَبَّكُمُ ٱلَّذِى خَلَقَكُم مِّن نَّفْسٍ وَٰحِدَةٍ وَخَلَقَ مِنْهَا زَوْجَهَا وَبَثَّ مِنْهُمَا رِجَالًا كَثِيرًا وَنِسَآءً ۚ وَٱتَّقُوا۟ ٱللَّهَ ٱلَّذِى تَسَآءَلُونَ بِهِۦ وَٱلْأَرْحَامَ ۚ إِنَّ ٱللَّهَ كَانَ عَلَيْكُمْ رَقِيبًا ۝١}$$

O you who have believed, fear Allah and speak words of appropriate justice. (33:70)

$$\text{يَٰٓأَيُّهَا ٱلَّذِينَ ءَامَنُوا۟ ٱتَّقُوا۟ ٱللَّهَ وَقُولُوا۟ قَوْلًا سَدِيدًا ۝٧٠}$$

He will [then] amend for you your deeds and forgive you your sins. And whoever obeys Allah and His Messenger has certainly attained a great attainment. (33:71)

$$\text{يُصْلِحْ لَكُمْ أَعْمَٰلَكُمْ وَيَغْفِرْ لَكُمْ ذُنُوبَكُمْ ۗ وَمَن يُطِعِ ٱللَّهَ وَرَسُولَهُۥ فَقَدْ فَازَ فَوْزًا عَظِيمًا ۝٧١}$$

Hypocrisy is a deep rooted and all-pervading spiritual illness. It is a bad disease. A person's heart could be overflowing with it yet be oblivious of it due to its hidden nature;

frequently it leads a person to think he is acting righty when in reality he is spreading corruption. It is of two types: major and minor; major hypocrisy leads to eternal punishment in the lowest depths of Hell; it is to outwardly display faith in Allah, His Angels, His Books, His Messengers and the Last Day.

Whereas inwardly one is devoid of such belief, indeed disbelieving in it. He does not believe that Allah spoke to a man amongst men who He appointed to be a Messenger: guiding them by His permission and warning them of His punishment. If they had believed and **feared Allah** then the reward from **Allah** would have been [far] better, if they only knew. (2:103)

$$\text{وَلَوْ أَنَّهُمْ ءَامَنُوا۟ وَٱتَّقَوْا۟ لَمَثُوبَةٌ مِّنْ عِندِ ٱللَّهِ خَيْرٌ لَّوْ كَانُوا۟ يَعْلَمُونَ ۝}$$

In the Quran, Allah has revealed the machinations of the hypocrites, He has unveiled their beliefs, their qualities, and made their goals clear so that the believers can be aware of them. Indeed, the hypocrites will be in the lowest depths of the Fire - and never will you find for them a helper. (4:145)

$$\text{إِنَّ ٱلْمُنَٰفِقِينَ فِى ٱلدَّرْكِ ٱلْأَسْفَلِ مِنَ ٱلنَّارِ وَلَن تَجِدَ لَهُمْ نَصِيرًا ۝}$$

Allah divided mankind into three different groups in the beginning of Surah al- Baqarah (the Cow):

The **believer**, the **disbeliever**, and the **hypocrite**.

Allah related 4 verses concerning the believers, 2 verses concerning the disbelievers, & 13 verses concerning the hypocrites due to their plenitude and the great harm and tribulation they bring to Islam and the Muslims.

The harm they cause to Islam is truly severe for they claim to be Muslims, they claim to aid and support Islam, whereas in reality they are its enemies seeking to destroy it from within, covertly spreading their corruption and ignorance such that the unwary thinks that what they are upon is knowledge and right action. How many strongholds of Islam have they destroyed; how many fortresses have they rendered to ruin; how many sign-posts of Islam have they effaced; how many raised flags have they lowered; and how many seeds of doubt have they attempted to sow in order to uproot the religion!

Islam and the Muslims have always faced trial and tribulation from them, wave after wave of doubts do they assault at it, all the while thinking that they are doing right.

Unquestionably, it is they who are the corrupters, but they perceive [it] not. (2:12)

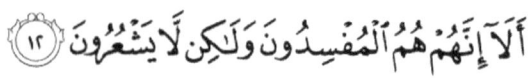

Allah, Exalted is He says: They hypocrites are apprehensive lest a surah be revealed about them, informing them of what is in their hearts. Say, "Mock [as you wish]; indeed, Allah will expose that which you fear." (9:64)

يَحْذَرُ ٱلْمُنَٰفِقُونَ أَن تُنَزَّلَ عَلَيْهِمْ سُورَةٌ تُنَبِّئُهُم بِمَا فِى قُلُوبِهِمْ ۚ قُلِ ٱسْتَهْزِءُوٓا۟ إِنَّ ٱللَّهَ مُخْرِجٌ مَّا تَحْذَرُونَ ﴿٦٤﴾

They desire to extinguish the light of Allah with their mouths, but Allah will perfect His light, although the disbelievers hate it. (61:8)

يُرِيدُونَ لِيُطْفِـُٔوا۟ نُورَ ٱللَّهِ بِأَفْوَٰهِهِمْ وَٱللَّهُ مُتِمُّ نُورِهِۦ وَلَوْ كَرِهَ ٱلْكَٰفِرُونَ ﴿٨﴾

They want to abandon the revelation and follow a course other than the one directed by it.

But they disagreed and split up. They (have broken their religion among them into sects, each group rejoicing in its belief. (23:53)

فَتَقَطَّعُوٓا۟ أَمْرَهُم بَيْنَهُمْ زُبُرًا ۖ كُلُّ حِزْبٍۭ بِمَا لَدَيْهِمْ فَرِحُونَ ۝

And thus We have made for every prophet an enemy - devils from mankind and jinn, inspiring to one another decorative speech in delusion. But if your Lord had willed, they would not have done it, so leave them and that which they invent. (6:112)

وَكَذَٰلِكَ جَعَلْنَا لِكُلِّ نَبِىٍّ عَدُوًّا شَيَٰطِينَ ٱلْإِنسِ وَٱلْجِنِّ يُوحِى بَعْضُهُمْ إِلَىٰ بَعْضٍ زُخْرُفَ ٱلْقَوْلِ غُرُورًا ۚ وَلَوْ شَآءَ رَبُّكَ مَا فَعَلُوهُ ۖ فَذَرْهُمْ وَمَا يَفْتَرُونَ ۝

And because of this, the Messenger has said: "O my Lord, indeed my people have taken this Qur'an as [a thing] abandoned." (25:30)

وَقَالَ ٱلرَّسُولُ يَـٰرَبِّ إِنَّ قَوْمِى ٱتَّخَذُواْ هَـٰذَا ٱلْقُرْءَانَ مَهْجُورًا ﴿٣٠﴾

They took this Quran as something to be ignored.

The characteristics of faith are not to be found in their hearts and hence they do not know then; oblivious are they to its pillars and hence do not take care of them; extinguished are the brilliant lights of its stars in their hearts and they do not try to relight them, and the darkness of their thoughts and beliefs has eclipsed the sun of faith such that they no longer see it.

They do not accept the guidance of Allah with which He sent His

Messengers, they attach no importance to it, and they see nothing wrong in leaving it for their own opinions and beliefs. They have wrenched the texts of revelation of their true status, they have detached them of their importance and definitiveness, and they have submerged them in the obscurity of false interpretations.

Subterfuge after subterfuge do they launch against these texts, and it is as if they face them in the same way an unwilling host meets malevolent guests: devoid of acceptance and generosity, all the while forcing himself to host them, yet keeping his distance. They say to these texts: "You have no way to pass by us, and if they find no option but to accept them," they do so by propounding various plots. When these texts find way past their doors, they say: "what have we to do with their literal meanings, they give us no certainty whatsoever!" And the general masses amongst them say: "Sufficient for us is what we find the latter people upon for they were more knowledgeable than the Righteous Predecessors, and firmer and more rightly guided in knowing the proofs and evidences!"

In their view the way of the Salaf is the way of simplicity and soundness of heart because they did not busy themselves with investigating and laying out the principles of rhetoric; instead they simply devoted themselves to doing the obligatory and leaving the prohibited. Therefore the way of the latter people is more deeply rooted in knowledge and wiser whereas the way of the Salaf is greater in ignorance but safer.

They treat the texts of the Book and Sunnah like the Khalifah is treated in these times: while his name is written on coins and gains superficial mention in the Friday sermons, he has no real authority and it is other men who govern, his judgment is neither heard nor adhered to.

They have donned the robes of the people of faith which cover their hearts of misguidance, deception and disbelief. Their tongues are the tongues of Muslims but their hearts are the hearts of those fighting them. They say: And of the people are some who say, "We believe in Allah and the Last Day," but they are not believers. (2:8)

﴿وَمِنَ ٱلنَّاسِ مَن يَقُولُ ءَامَنَّا بِٱللَّهِ وَبِٱلْيَوْمِ ٱلْأَخِرِ وَمَا هُم بِمُؤْمِنِينَ ۝﴾

They [think to] deceive Allah and those who believe, but they deceive not except themselves and perceive [it] not.

$$\text{يُخَٰدِعُونَ ٱللَّهَ وَٱلَّذِينَ ءَامَنُواْ وَمَا يَخْدَعُونَ إِلَّآ أَنفُسَهُمْ وَمَا يَشْعُرُونَ ۝}$$

Look how they invent about Allah untruth, and sufficient is that as a manifest sin. (4:50)

$$\text{ٱنظُرْ كَيْفَ يَفْتَرُونَ عَلَى ٱللَّهِ ٱلْكَذِبَّ وَكَفَىٰ بِهِۦٓ إِثْمًا مُّبِينًا ۝}$$

Their capital is deception and scheming, their merchandise is lies and treachery, and their intellect is one that is employed just for this world: believers and disbelievers alike are happy with them and they live in security amongst both.

The disease of desires and doubts has consumed their hearts and destroyed them, and evil objectives have permeated their motivations and intentions and corrupted them.

Their corruption is so severe that they are flung to perdition, and the doctors of the religion are unable to cure them. And let not those who disbelieve ever think that [because] We extend their time [of enjoyment] it is better for them. We only extend it for them so that they may increase in sin, and for them is a humiliating punishment (3:178)

وَلَا يَحْسَبَنَّ ٱلَّذِينَ كَفَرُوٓا۟ أَنَّمَا نُمْلِى لَهُمْ خَيْرٌ لِّأَنفُسِهِمْ ۚ إِنَّمَا نُمْلِى لَهُمْ لِيَزْدَادُوٓا۟ إِثْمًا ۚ وَلَهُمْ عَذَابٌ مُّهِينٌ ۝

On the [same] Day the hypocrite men and hypocrite women will say to those who believed, "Wait for us that we may acquire some of your light." It will be said, "Go back behind you and seek light." And a wall will be placed between them with a door, its interior containing mercy, but on the outside of it is torment. (57:13)

يَوْمَ يَقُولُ ٱلْمُنَٰفِقُونَ وَٱلْمُنَٰفِقَٰتُ لِلَّذِينَ ءَامَنُوا۟ ٱنظُرُونَا نَقْتَبِسْ مِن نُّورِكُمْ قِيلَ ٱرْجِعُوا۟ وَرَآءَكُمْ فَٱلْتَمِسُوا۟ نُورًا فَضُرِبَ بَيْنَهُم بِسُورٍ لَّهُۥ بَابٌۢ بَاطِنُهُۥ فِيهِ ٱلرَّحْمَةُ وَظَٰهِرُهُۥ مِن قِبَلِهِ ٱلْعَذَابُ ۝١٣

In their hearts is disease, so Allah has increased their disease; and for them is a very painful punishment because they [habitually] used to lie. (2:10)

فِى قُلُوبِهِم مَّرَضٌ فَزَادَهُمُ ٱللَّهُ مَرَضًا ۖ وَلَهُمْ عَذَابٌ أَلِيمٌۢ بِمَا كَانُوا۟ يَكْذِبُونَ ۝١٠

Whoever falls prey to the claws of their doubts will have his faith shredded to pieces; whoever allows his heart to open to their vile tribulations will find himself in a burning furnace; and whoever lends an ear to their deceptions will find them coming between him and firm belief. Indeed the corruption they cause on earth is great but most people are unaware.

And whenever a surah is revealed, there are among the hypocrites those who say, "Which of you has this increased faith?" As for those who believed, it has increased them in faith, while they are rejoicing. (9:124)

وَإِذَا مَا أُنزِلَتْ سُورَةٌ فَمِنْهُم مَّن يَقُولُ أَيُّكُمْ زَادَتْهُ هَٰذِهِۦٓ إِيمَٰنًا ۚ فَأَمَّا ٱلَّذِينَ ءَامَنُوا۟ فَزَادَتْهُمْ إِيمَٰنًا وَهُمْ يَسْتَبْشِرُونَ ﴿١٢٤﴾

But as for those in whose hearts is disease, it has [only] increased them in evil [in addition] to their evil. And they will have died while they are disbelievers.

$$وَأَمَّا ٱلَّذِينَ فِى قُلُوبِهِم مَّرَضٌ فَزَادَتْهُمْ رِجْسًا إِلَىٰ رِجْسِهِمْ وَمَاتُوا۟ وَهُمْ كَٰفِرُونَ ﴿١٢٥﴾$$

And when it is said to them, "Do not cause corruption on the earth," they say, "We are but reformers." (2:11)

$$وَإِذَا قِيلَ لَهُمْ لَا تُفْسِدُوا۟ فِى ٱلْأَرْضِ قَالُوٓا۟ إِنَّمَا نَحْنُ مُصْلِحُونَ ﴿١١﴾$$

Unquestionably, it is they who are the corrupters, but they perceive [it] not.

أَلَا إِنَّهُمْ هُمُ ٱلْمُفْسِدُونَ وَلَٰكِن لَّا يَشْعُرُونَ ﴿١٢﴾

When they are told, Do not cause corruption on the earth, they say: "We are only putting things right. No indeed! They are the corrupters but they are not aware of it."

When one of them follows the Book and Sunnah, he is doing so to keep up appearances, he is like a donkey carrying books: it understands none of what it is carrying. The revelation in their eyes is profitless merchandise and as such worthless. Those who truly follow it are fools in their eyes.

And when it is said to them, "Believe as the people have believed," they say, "Should we believe as the foolish have believed?" Unquestionably, it is they who are the foolish, but they know [it] not. (2:13)

وَإِذَا قِيلَ لَهُمْ ءَامِنُواْ كَمَآ ءَامَنَ ٱلنَّاسُ قَالُوٓاْ أَنُؤْمِنُ كَمَآ ءَامَنَ ٱلسُّفَهَآءُ ۗ أَلَآ إِنَّهُمْ هُمُ ٱلسُّفَهَآءُ وَلَٰكِن لَّا يَعْلَمُونَ ۝

This verse describes their fifth characteristic: spreading corruption in the land, a direct consequence of the corruption of their hearts.

Each one of them has two faces: a face with which he meets the Muslims and a face with which he meets his deviated associates. Each one of them has two tongues: a false tongue with which he meets the Muslims and a true tongue which expresses his actual beliefs,

And when they meet those who believe, they say, "We believe"; but when they are alone with their evil ones, they say, "Indeed, we are with you; we were only mockers." (2:14)

وَإِذَا لَقُوا۟ ٱلَّذِينَ ءَامَنُوا۟ قَالُوٓا۟ ءَامَنَّا وَإِذَا خَلَوْا۟ إِلَىٰ شَيَٰطِينِهِمْ قَالُوٓا۟ إِنَّا مَعَكُمْ إِنَّمَا نَحْنُ مُسْتَهْزِءُونَ ۝

This describes the 6th characteristic: their belittling the religion and those who follow it, and their foolishness. Allah informs us that they are the true fools because foolishness is defined by a person not knowing what is good for himself and his pursuing that which would harm him. These qualities are applicable to them. They way of intelligence and insight is for a person to know what is good for him and to pursue it and to repress what would harm him. These qualities are applicable to the Companions and the believers. Consideration is given to reality and not to mere claims and empty words. They conceal [their evil intentions and deeds] from the people, but they cannot conceal [them] from Allah, and He is with them [in His knowledge] when they spend the night in such as He does not accept of speech. And ever is Allah, of what they do, encompassing. (4:108)

يَسْتَخْفُونَ مِنَ ٱلنَّاسِ وَلَا يَسْتَخْفُونَ مِنَ ٱللَّهِ وَهُوَ مَعَهُمْ إِذْ يُبَيِّتُونَ مَا لَا يَرْضَىٰ مِنَ ٱلْقَوْلِ ۚ وَكَانَ ٱللَّهُ بِمَا يَعْمَلُونَ مُحِيطًا ﴿١٠٨﴾

They have turned away from the Book and Sunnah, making mockery of those who follow them and looking down on them. They refuse to submit to the revelation, making do with what knowledge they have: and what knowledge? The increase of which only leads to more evil and arrogance! You will always see them mocking those who follow the clear import of the revelation but,

[But] Allah mocks them and prolongs them in their transgression [while] they wander blindly. (2:15)

ٱللَّهُ يَسْتَهْزِئُ بِهِمْ وَيَمُدُّهُمْ فِى طُغْيَٰنِهِمْ يَعْمَهُونَ ۝

They practice their trade in oceans of darkness traversing vessels of doubts.

Uncertainty and suspicion plagues them as they sail through waves of illusion. Strong winds play havoc with their boats and lead them to their destruction. Those are the ones who have purchased error [in exchange] for guidance, so their transaction has brought no profit, nor were they guided. (2:16)

أُولَٰئِكَ ٱلَّذِينَ ٱشْتَرَوُاْ ٱلضَّلَٰلَةَ بِٱلْهُدَىٰ فَمَا رَبِحَت تِّجَٰرَتُهُمْ وَمَا كَانُواْ مُهْتَدِينَ ﴿١٦﴾

Allah, Exalted is He says: And it has already come down to you in the Book that when you hear the verses of Allah [recited], they are denied [by them] and ridiculed; so do not sit with them until they enter into another conversation. Indeed, you would then be like them. Indeed Allah will gather the hypocrites and disbelievers in Hell. (4:140)

وَقَدْ نَزَّلَ عَلَيْكُمْ فِى ٱلْكِتَٰبِ أَنْ إِذَا سَمِعْتُمْ ءَايَٰتِ ٱللَّهِ يُكْفَرُ بِهَا وَيُسْتَهْزَأُ بِهَا فَلَا تَقْعُدُواْ مَعَهُمْ حَتَّىٰ يَخُوضُواْ فِى حَدِيثٍ غَيْرِهِۦٓ إِنَّكُمْ إِذًا مِّثْلُهُمْ إِنَّ ٱللَّهَ جَامِعُ ٱلْمُنَٰفِقِينَ وَٱلْكَٰفِرِينَ فِى جَهَنَّمَ جَمِيعًا ﴿١٤٠﴾

The fire of faith alights for them and in its light they perceive guidance and misguidance, then that fire is extinguished and is left as red hot ashes. With that fire are they punished and in that darkness do they wander blindly,

Their example is that of one who kindled a fire, but when it illuminated what was around him, Allah took away their light and left them in darkness [so] they could not see. (2:17)

مَثَلُهُمْ كَمَثَلِ ٱلَّذِى ٱسْتَوْقَدَ نَارًا فَلَمَّآ أَضَآءَتْ مَا حَوْلَهُۥ ذَهَبَ ٱللَّهُ بِنُورِهِمْ وَتَرَكَهُمْ فِى ظُلُمَٰتٍ لَّا يُبْصِرُونَ ﴿١٧﴾

The hearing of their hearts is burdened by a heavy load and as such they are unable to hear the call to faith; the eyes of their spiritual sight are covered with a blinding wrapping such that they cannot see the realities of the Quran; and dleir tongues are mute to the truth such that they are unable to speak it. Deaf, dumb and blind - so they will not return [to the right path]. (2:18)

$$صُمٌّ بُكْمٌ عُمْىٌ فَهُمْ لَا يَرْجِعُونَ ۝$$

And if you could but see when the angels take the souls of those who disbelieved... They are striking their faces and their backs and [saying], "Taste the punishment of the Burning Fire. (8:50)

$$وَلَوْ تَرَىٰ إِذْ يَتَوَفَّى ٱلَّذِينَ كَفَرُواْ ٱلْمَلَٰٓئِكَةُ يَضْرِبُونَ وُجُوهَهُمْ وَأَدْبَٰرَهُمْ وَذُوقُواْ عَذَابَ ٱلْحَرِيقِ ۝$$

The rain of revelation pours down upon them, it contains life for the hearts and souls, but all they can hear of it is the thunder strikes of its threats, promises, and ordinances.

They thrust their fingers in their ears and draw their garments over them, trying to run in earnest and desperately seeking their footprints so as to retreat. However they are summoned in public, and their secrets are made plain for all who can see, and two parables are propounded for them, each parable unveiling one of the two parties amongst them: those who debate and those who blindly follow. Or [it is] like a rainstorm from the sky within which is darkness, thunder and lightning. They put their fingers in their ears against the thunderclaps in dread of death. But Allah is encompassing of the disbelievers. (2:19)

أَوْ كَصَيِّبٍ مِّنَ ٱلسَّمَآءِ فِيهِ ظُلُمَٰتٌ وَرَعْدٌ وَبَرْقٌ يَجْعَلُونَ أَصَٰبِعَهُمْ فِىٓ ءَاذَانِهِم مِّنَ ٱلصَّوَٰعِقِ حَذَرَ ٱلْمَوْتِ ۚ وَٱللَّهُ مُحِيطٌۢ بِٱلْكَٰفِرِينَ ۝١٩

Their spiritual sight is too weak to bear what the rain contains: the lightning of its radiant proofs and the brightness of its mean- ings. Their ears are unable to accept the thunder strikes of its promises, orders, and prohibitions; as such they come to a halt in confusion, their faculty of hearing brings them no benefit and their sight is unable to guide them.

The lightning almost snatches away their sight. Every time it lights [the way] for them, they walk therein; but when darkness comes over them, they stand [still]. And if Allah had willed, He could have taken away their hearing and their sight. Indeed, Allah is over all things competent. (2:20)

يَكَادُ ٱلْبَرْقُ يَخْطَفُ أَبْصَٰرَهُمْ ۖ كُلَّمَاۤ أَضَآءَ لَهُم مَّشَوْا۟ فِيهِ وَإِذَاۤ أَظْلَمَ عَلَيْهِمْ قَامُوا۟ ۚ وَلَوْ شَآءَ ٱللَّهُ لَذَهَبَ بِسَمْعِهِمْ وَأَبْصَٰرِهِمْ ۚ إِنَّ ٱللَّهَ عَلَىٰ كُلِّ شَىْءٍ قَدِيرٌ ۝٢٠

They have characteristic signs by which they can be known, explained in the Book and the Sunnah, and clear for all those who are enriched with faith to see. They are people, by Allah, given to ostentation, and this is the worst station that man can reach. They are a people prone to laziness and laxity in fulfilling the orders of the All-Merciful, and because of this they find sincerity burdensome.

Indeed, the hypocrites [think to] deceive Allah, but He is deceiving them. And when they stand for prayer, they stand lazily, showing [themselves to] the people and not remembering Allah except a little. (4:142)

إِنَّ ٱلْمُنَٰفِقِينَ يُخَٰدِعُونَ ٱللَّهَ وَهُوَ خَٰدِعُهُمْ وَإِذَا قَامُوٓا۟ إِلَى ٱلصَّلَوٰةِ قَامُوا۟ كُسَالَىٰ يُرَآءُونَ ٱلنَّاسَ وَلَا يَذْكُرُونَ ٱللَّهَ إِلَّا قَلِيلًا ﴿١٤٢﴾

They ate like a sheep that has strayed and finds itself between two flocks, it goes to one and then the other and does not stay with any of them. They are standing between two groups of people, all the while searching as to which is the stronger and nobler.

Wavering between them, [belonging] neither to the believers nor to the disbelievers. And whoever Allah leaves astray - never will you find for him a way. (4:143)

مُّذَبْذَبِينَ بَيْنَ ذَٰلِكَ لَا إِلَىٰ هَٰؤُلَاءِ وَلَا إِلَىٰ هَٰؤُلَاءِ ۚ وَمَن يُضْلِلِ اللَّهُ فَلَن تَجِدَ لَهُ سَبِيلًا ﴿١٤٣﴾

They are on the lookout to see what happens to Ahlus-Sunnah; if victory comes their way they say: Were we not with you? And they swear their strongest oaths by Allah on this. If victory goes to the enemies of Ahlus-Sunnah they say to them 'Do you not know that we have a binding pact of brotherhood with you' and they bring their closeness of lineage as proof for this. Allah also says about them: And what prevents their expenditures from being accepted from them but that they have disbelieved in Allah and in His Messenger and that they come not to prayer except while they are lazy and that they do not spend but while they are unwilling. (9:54)

وَمَا مَنَعَهُمْ أَن تُقْبَلَ مِنْهُمْ نَفَقَـٰتُهُمْ إِلَّا أَنَّهُمْ كَفَرُوا۟ بِٱللَّهِ وَبِرَسُولِهِۦ وَلَا يَأْتُونَ ٱلصَّلَوٰةَ إِلَّا وَهُمْ كُسَالَىٰ وَلَا يُنفِقُونَ إِلَّا وَهُمْ كَـٰرِهُونَ ۝

Whoever wishes to know them, let him take their descriptions from the words of the Lord of the worlds, and after that he will require no further proof.

Those who wait [and watch] you. Then if you gain a victory from Allah, they say, "Were we not with you?" But if the disbelievers have a success, they say [to them], "Did we not gain the advantage over you, but we protected you from the believers?" Allah will judge between [all of] you on the Day of Resurrection, and never will Allah give the disbelievers over the believers a way [to overcome them]. (4:141)

ٱلَّذِينَ يَتَرَبَّصُونَ بِكُمْ فَإِن كَانَ لَكُمْ فَتْحٌ مِّنَ ٱللَّهِ قَالُوٓاْ أَلَمْ نَكُن مَّعَكُمْ وَإِن كَانَ لِلْكَٰفِرِينَ نَصِيبٌ قَالُوٓاْ أَلَمْ نَسْتَحْوِذْ عَلَيْكُمْ وَنَمْنَعْكُم مِّنَ ٱلْمُؤْمِنِينَ فَٱللَّهُ يَحْكُمُ بَيْنَكُمْ يَوْمَ ٱلْقِيَٰمَةِ وَلَن يَجْعَلَ ٱللَّهُ لِلْكَٰفِرِينَ عَلَى ٱلْمُؤْمِنِينَ سَبِيلًا ۝

One who listens to them will be astounded by the silkiness and softness of their speech, he will bring Allah to witness for what is in his heart of lies and deceit.

And of the people is he whose speech pleases you in worldly life, and he calls Allah to witness as to what is in his heart, yet he is the fiercest of opponents. (2:204)

وَمِنَ ٱلنَّاسِ مَن يُعْجِبُكَ قَوْلُهُۥ فِى ٱلْحَيَوٰةِ ٱلدُّنْيَا وَيُشْهِدُ ٱللَّهَ عَلَىٰ مَا فِى قَلْبِهِۦ وَهُوَ أَلَدُّ ٱلْخِصَامِ ۝

O you who have believed, do not take the Jews and the Christians as allies. They are [in fact] allies of one another. And whoever is an ally to them among you - then indeed, he is [one] of them. Indeed, Allah guides not the wrongdoing people. (5:51-52)

$$\text{۞ يَٰٓأَيُّهَا ٱلَّذِينَ ءَامَنُوا۟ لَا تَتَّخِذُوا۟ ٱلْيَهُودَ وَٱلنَّصَٰرَىٰٓ أَوْلِيَآءَ ۘ بَعْضُهُمْ أَوْلِيَآءُ بَعْضٍ ۚ وَمَن يَتَوَلَّهُم مِّنكُمْ فَإِنَّهُۥ مِنْهُمْ ۗ إِنَّ ٱللَّهَ لَا يَهْدِى ٱلْقَوْمَ ٱلظَّٰلِمِينَ ۝٥١}$$

So you see those in whose hearts is disease hastening into [association with] them, saying, "We are afraid a misfortune may strike us." But perhaps Allah will bring conquest or a decision from Him, and they will become, over what they have been concealing within themselves, regretful.

$$\text{فَتَرَى ٱلَّذِينَ فِى قُلُوبِهِم مَّرَضٌ يُسَٰرِعُونَ فِيهِمْ يَقُولُونَ نَخْشَىٰٓ أَن تُصِيبَنَا دَآئِرَةٌ ۚ فَعَسَى ٱللَّهُ أَن يَأْتِىَ بِٱلْفَتْحِ أَوْ أَمْرٍ مِّنْ عِندِهِۦ فَيُصْبِحُوا۟ عَلَىٰ مَآ أَسَرُّوا۟ فِىٓ أَنفُسِهِمْ نَٰدِمِينَ ۝٥٢}$$

What they enjoin upon their followers entails corrupting them and spreading corruption in the land. What they prohibit their followers from entails what would be better for them in this life and the Hereafter. You would see one of them amongst the believers praying & remembering Allah.

And when he goes away, he strives throughout the land to cause corruption therein and destroy crops and animals. And Allah does not like corruption. (2:205)

وَإِذَا تَوَلَّىٰ سَعَىٰ فِى ٱلْأَرْضِ لِيُفْسِدَ فِيهَا وَيُهْلِكَ ٱلْحَرْثَ وَٱلنَّسْلَ ۗ وَٱللَّهُ لَا يُحِبُّ ٱلْفَسَادَ ۝

They are all similar, enjoining the evil after having committed it themselves and prohibiting the good after having left it themselves. They are miserly in giving their wealth in the way of Allah, in ways that He loves it to be spent. How many times has Allah reminded them of the blessings He has conferred upon them yet they turn away and abandon Him! Listen, believers, to what He says about them.

Worship Allah and associate nothing with Him, and to parents do good, and to relatives, orphans, the needy, the near neighbor, the neighbor farther away, the companion at your side, the traveler, and those whom your right hands possess. Indeed, Allah does not like those who are self-deluding and boastful. (4:36-37)

۞ وَٱعۡبُدُوا۟ ٱللَّهَ وَلَا تُشۡرِكُوا۟ بِهِۦ شَيۡـًٔاۖ وَبِٱلۡوَٰلِدَيۡنِ إِحۡسَـٰنًا وَبِذِى ٱلۡقُرۡبَىٰ وَٱلۡيَتَـٰمَىٰ وَٱلۡمَسَـٰكِينِ وَٱلۡجَارِ ذِى ٱلۡقُرۡبَىٰ وَٱلۡجَارِ ٱلۡجُنُبِ وَٱلصَّاحِبِ بِٱلۡجَنۢبِ وَٱبۡنِ ٱلسَّبِيلِ وَمَا مَلَكَتۡ أَيۡمَـٰنُكُمۡۗ إِنَّ ٱللَّهَ لَا يُحِبُّ مَن كَانَ مُخۡتَالًا فَخُورًا ﴿٣٦﴾

Who are stingy and enjoin upon [other] people stinginess and conceal what Allah has given them of His bounty - and We have prepared for the disbelievers a humiliating punishment.

ٱلَّذِينَ يَبۡخَلُونَ وَيَأۡمُرُونَ ٱلنَّاسَ بِٱلۡبُخۡلِ وَيَكۡتُمُونَ مَآ ءَاتَىٰهُمُ ٱللَّهُ مِن فَضۡلِهِۦۗ وَأَعۡتَدۡنَا لِلۡكَـٰفِرِينَ عَذَابًا مُّهِينًا ﴿٣٧﴾

If you invite them to judge by the clear import of the revelation you will see them turn away in aversion. If you could see their reality you would see a vast gulf between them and the truth, and you would see the stringency with which they turn away from the revelation.

The hypocrite men and hypocrite women are of one another. They enjoin what is wrong and forbid what is right and close their hands. They have forgotten Allah, so He has forgotten them [accordingly]. Indeed, the hypocrites - it is they who are the defiantly disobedient. (9:67)

ٱلْمُنَٰفِقُونَ وَٱلْمُنَٰفِقَٰتُ بَعْضُهُم مِّنۢ بَعْضٍ ۚ يَأْمُرُونَ بِٱلْمُنكَرِ وَيَنْهَوْنَ عَنِ ٱلْمَعْرُوفِ وَيَقْبِضُونَ أَيْدِيَهُمْ ۚ نَسُوا۟ ٱللَّهَ فَنَسِيَهُمْ ۗ إِنَّ ٱلْمُنَٰفِقِينَ هُمُ ٱلْفَٰسِقُونَ ﴿٦٧﴾

And when it is said to them, "Come to what Allah has revealed and to the Messenger," you see the hypocrites turning away from you in aversion. (4:61)

وَإِذَا قِيلَ لَهُمْ تَعَالَوْا۟ إِلَىٰ مَآ أَنزَلَ ٱللَّهُ وَإِلَى ٱلرَّسُولِ رَأَيْتَ ٱلْمُنَٰفِقِينَ يَصُدُّونَ عَنكَ صُدُودًا ﴿٦١﴾

How can they be successful and guided after their intellects and religion have been afflicted so, truly unlikely is it that they will be saved from the mire and misguidance they are in. They have bought disbelief at the expense of faith and what trade is there as profitless as this?! They have exchanged the choicest sealed wine for blazing fire.

So how [will it be] when disaster strikes them because of what their hands have put forth and then they come to you swearing by Allah, "We intended nothing but good conduct and accommodation." (4:62)

فَكَيْفَ إِذَآ أَصَٰبَتْهُم مُّصِيبَةٌۢ بِمَا قَدَّمَتْ أَيْدِيهِمْ ثُمَّ جَآءُوكَ يَحْلِفُونَ بِٱللَّهِ إِنْ أَرَدْنَآ إِلَّآ إِحْسَٰنًا وَتَوْفِيقًا ۝

The vileness of doubts and suspicion cling firmly to their hearts and they can find no way of absolution from them.

Have you not seen those who claim to have believed in what was revealed to you, [O Muhammad], and what was revealed before you? They wish to refer legislation to Taghut, while they were commanded to reject it; and Satan wishes to lead them far astray. (4:60)

أَلَمْ تَرَ إِلَى ٱلَّذِينَ يَزْعُمُونَ أَنَّهُمْ ءَامَنُوا۟ بِمَآ أُنزِلَ إِلَيْكَ وَمَآ أُنزِلَ مِن قَبْلِكَ يُرِيدُونَ أَن يَتَحَاكَمُوٓا۟ إِلَى ٱلطَّٰغُوتِ وَقَدْ أُمِرُوٓا۟ أَن يَكْفُرُوا۟ بِهِۦ وَيُرِيدُ ٱلشَّيْطَٰنُ أَن يُضِلَّهُمْ ضَلَٰلًۢا بَعِيدًا ۝

Those are the ones of whom Allah knows what is in their hearts, so turn away from them but admonish them and speak to them a far-reaching word. (4:63

أُوْلَٰٓئِكَ ٱلَّذِينَ يَعْلَمُ ٱللَّهُ مَا فِى قُلُوبِهِمْ فَأَعْرِضْ عَنْهُمْ وَعِظْهُمْ وَقُل لَّهُمْ فِىٓ أَنفُسِهِمْ قَوْلًۢا بَلِيغًا ۝

May they perish! How distant they are from the reality of faith! They are one thing and the followers of the Messenger (peace be upon him) are something totally different.

Allah, Mighty and Magnificent, has taken an oath in His Book upon Himself; the greatness of which will be realized by those endowed with spiritual insight, those whose hearts are fearful of Him by way of magnification and exaltation.

Allah, Exalted is He, says: warning His friends and alerting us to the state of these people.

But no, by your Lord, they will not [truly] believe until they make you, [O Muhammad], judge concerning that over which they dispute among themselves and then find within themselves no discomfort from what you have judged and submit in [full, willing] submission. (4:65)

فَلَا وَرَبِّكَ لَا يُؤْمِنُونَ حَتَّىٰ يُحَكِّمُوكَ فِيمَا شَجَرَ بَيْنَهُمْ ثُمَّ لَا يَجِدُوا فِي أَنفُسِهِمْ حَرَجًا مِّمَّا قَضَيْتَ وَيُسَلِّمُوا تَسْلِيمًا ﴿٦٥﴾

You will find one of them taking oaths before commencing his words, without anyone even objecting to what he says: because he knows that the hearts of the believers do not find tranquility in what he says.

Therefore he uses the oath as a way of securing himself from any suspicions that may come his way. It is in the same way that people given to doubts and misgivings lie, making oaths in order to beguile the listener into thinking they are telling the truth.

They have taken their oaths as a cover, so they averted [people] from the way of Allah. Indeed, it was evil that they were doing. (63:2)

ٱتَّخَذُوٓاْ أَيْمَٰنَهُمْ جُنَّةً فَصَدُّواْ عَن سَبِيلِ ٱللَّهِ إِنَّهُمْ سَآءَ مَا كَانُواْ يَعْمَلُونَ ۝

May they perish! They embarked upon the journey across the great white plain with the caravan of faith, then seeing the length of the journey and how far its destination was, they turned on their heels and returned. They think they have found a good life, and they sleep comfortably in their beds, but neither in that life have they really lived, and neither in that slumber have they found any real benefit. It is not long till when a caller will give a single cry and they will all stand forth, leaving their life behind, hungry, not feeling any form of satiation... what will their state be at the time of the Meeting? They knew then they rejected, they saw the truth then they became blinded to it.

They swear by Allah to you [Muslims] to satisfy you. But Allah and His Messenger are more worthy for them to satisfy, if they should be believers. (9:62-63)

يَحْلِفُونَ بِٱللَّهِ لَكُمْ لِيُرْضُوكُمْ وَٱللَّهُ وَرَسُولُهُۥٓ أَحَقُّ أَن يُرْضُوهُ إِن كَانُوا۟ مُؤْمِنِينَ ۝

Do they not know that whoever opposes Allah and His Messenger - that for him is the fire of Hell, wherein he will abide eternally? That is the great disgrace.

ٱلَمْ يَعْلَمُوٓا۟ أَنَّهُۥ مَن يُحَادِدِ ٱللَّهَ وَرَسُولَهُۥ فَأَنَّ لَهُۥ نَارَ جَهَنَّمَ خَٰلِدًا فِيهَاۚ ذَٰلِكَ ٱلْخِزْىُ ٱلْعَظِيمُ ۝

That is because they believed, and then they disbelieved; so their hearts were sealed over, and they do not understand. (63:3)

ذَٰلِكَ بِأَنَّهُمْ ءَامَنُوا۟ ثُمَّ كَفَرُوا۟ فَطُبِعَ عَلَىٰ قُلُوبِهِمْ فَهُمْ لَا يَفْقَهُونَ ۝

The best of men in physical appearance, the most enchanting of tongues, the nicest words, yet the vilest of hearts. They are like propped up planks of wood devoid of fruit.

They have been severed from the source of their growth and as such rest on a wall to keep them upright so that people do not walk over them.

And when you see them, their forms please you, and if they speak, you listen to their speech. [They are] as if they were pieces of wood propped up - they think that every shout is against them. They are the enemy, so beware of them. May Allah destroy them; how are they deluded? (63:4)

۞ وَإِذَا رَأَيْتَهُمْ تُعْجِبُكَ أَجْسَامُهُمْ وَإِن يَقُولُوا تَسْمَعْ لِقَوْلِهِمْ كَأَنَّهُمْ خُشُبٌ مُّسَنَّدَةٌ يَحْسَبُونَ كُلَّ صَيْحَةٍ عَلَيْهِمْ هُمُ الْعَدُوُّ فَاحْذَرْهُمْ قَاتَلَهُمُ اللَّهُ أَنَّىٰ يُؤْفَكُونَ ﴿٤﴾

They delay the prayer to the last possible time: Fajr at sunrise and

Asr at sunset at which time they quickly peck the ground as does a crow.

This is because their prayer is a prayer in body but not of heart. While praying they look left and right as does a fox being certain that it is being hunted and chased. They do not attend the congregational prayer, rather they make do with praying in their homes or shops.

When they argue they behave uncouthly, when they are entrusted with something they break the trust, when they speak they lie, and when they promise they break it. This is how they deal with creation and Creator. Read their descriptions in the beginning of Al-Mutaffiffin and the end of at-Tariq for none can describe to you the characteristics of someone better than one who knows him well.

O Messenger of Allah, strive against the disbelievers and the hypocrites and be harsh upon them. And their refuge is Hell, and wretched is the destination. (66:9)

$$\text{يَٰٓأَيُّهَا ٱلنَّبِىُّ جَٰهِدِ ٱلْكُفَّارَ وَٱلْمُنَٰفِقِينَ وَٱغْلُظْ عَلَيْهِمْ ۚ وَمَأْوَىٰهُمْ جَهَنَّمُ ۖ وَبِئْسَ ٱلْمَصِيرُ ﴿٩﴾}$$

They may think they are many but in reality they are few. They may think they are strong but in reality they are weak and despi- cable. They are ignoramuses thinking themselves high and mighty. They are misled about Allah for they are ignorant of His greatness.

And they swear by Allah that they are from among you while they are not from among you; but they are a people who are afraid. (9:56)

$$\text{وَيَحْلِفُونَ بِاللَّهِ إِنَّهُمْ لَمِنكُمْ وَمَا هُم مِّنكُمْ وَلَٰكِنَّهُمْ قَوْمٌ يَفْرَقُونَ ﴿٥٦﴾}$$

And when you call to prayer, they take it in ridicule and amusement. That is because they are a people who do not use reason. (5:58)

$$\text{وَإِذَا نَادَيْتُمْ إِلَى الصَّلَاةِ اتَّخَذُوهَا هُزُوًا وَلَعِبًا ۚ ذَٰلِكَ بِأَنَّهُمْ قَوْمٌ لَّا يَعْقِلُونَ ﴿٥٨﴾}$$

When Ahlus-Sunnah meet with easy times, aid and victory, hard does it bear down on them and depressed do they become; and when Ahlus-Sunnah meet with straitened times and are tried by Allah so that their sins may be expiated, jubilant do they become and exultant. This is their legacy and in no way do those who inherit from the Messenger (peace and blessings be upon him) compare to those who inherit from the hypocrites.

Say, "Never will we be struck except by what Allah has decreed for us; He is our protector." And upon Allah let the believers rely. (9:51-52)

قُل لَّن يُصِيبَنَآ إِلَّا مَا كَتَبَ ٱللَّهُ لَنَا هُوَ مَوْلَىٰنَا ۚ وَعَلَى ٱللَّهِ فَلْيَتَوَكَّلِ ٱلْمُؤْمِنُونَ ﴿٥١﴾

Say, "Do you await for us except one of the two best things while we await for you that Allah will afflict you with punishment from Himself or at our hands? So wait; indeed we, along with you, are waiting."

$$\text{قُلْ هَلْ تَرَبَّصُونَ بِنَا إِلَّا إِحْدَى الْحُسْنَيَيْنِ وَنَحْنُ نَتَرَبَّصُ بِكُمْ أَن يُصِيبَكُمُ اللَّهُ بِعَذَابٍ مِّنْ عِندِهِ أَوْ بِأَيْدِينَا فَتَرَبَّصُوا إِنَّا مَعَكُم مُّتَرَبِّصُونَ ﴿٥٢﴾}$$

If they could find a refuge or some caves or any place to enter [and hide], they would turn to it while they run heedlessly. (9:57)

$$\text{لَوْ يَجِدُونَ مَلْجَأً أَوْ مَغَارَاتٍ أَوْ مُدَّخَلًا لَّوَلَّوْا إِلَيْهِ وَهُمْ يَجْمَحُونَ ﴿٥٧﴾}$$

If good touches you, it distresses them; but if harm strikes you, they rejoice at it. And if you are patient and fear Allah, their plot will not harm you at all. Indeed, Allah is encompassing of all what they do. (3:120)

$$\text{إِن تَمْسَسْكُمْ حَسَنَةٌ تَسُؤْهُمْ وَإِن تُصِبْكُمْ سَيِّئَةٌ يَفْرَحُوا بِهَا ۖ وَإِن تَصْبِرُوا وَتَتَّقُوا لَا يَضُرُّكُمْ كَيْدُهُمْ شَيْئًا ۗ إِنَّ اللَّهَ بِمَا يَعْمَلُونَ مُحِيطٌ ۝١٢٠}$$

Allah abhors their obeying Him because of the filth of their hearts and impure intentions; as such He held them back and impeded them from obeying Him. He hates to have them close to Him and in His vicinity due to their love of His enemies; as such He distanced them and discarded them. They turned away from His revelation so He turned away from them and decreed misery for them. He judged them with pure justice and they have no hope for victory unless they become of the penitent.

And if they had intended to go forth, they would have prepared for it [some] preparation. But Allah disliked their being sent, so He kept them back, and they were told, "Remain [behind] with those who remain." (9:46)

﴿وَلَوْ أَرَادُوا الْخُرُوجَ لَأَعَدُّوا لَهُ عُدَّةً وَلَٰكِن كَرِهَ اللَّهُ انبِعَاثَهُمْ فَثَبَّطَهُمْ وَقِيلَ اقْعُدُوا مَعَ الْقَاعِدِينَ ﴾ (٤٦)

Indeed, the hypocrites will be in the lowest depths of the Fire - and never will you find for them a helper. (4:145-146)

إِنَّ الْمُنَافِقِينَ فِي الدَّرْكِ الْأَسْفَلِ مِنَ النَّارِ وَلَن تَجِدَ لَهُمْ نَصِيرًا ﴿١٤٥﴾

Except for those who repent, correct themselves, hold fast to Allah, and are sincere in their religion for Allah, for those will be with the believers. And Allah is going to give the believers a great reward.

إِلَّا ٱلَّذِينَ تَابُواْ وَأَصْلَحُواْ وَٱعْتَصَمُواْ بِٱللَّهِ وَأَخْلَصُواْ دِينَهُمْ لِلَّهِ فَأُوْلَٰٓئِكَ مَعَ ٱلْمُؤْمِنِينَۖ وَسَوْفَ يُؤْتِ ٱللَّهُ ٱلْمُؤْمِنِينَ أَجْرًا عَظِيمًا ﴿١٤٦﴾

Then He mentions the wisdom behind His doing what has previously been mentioned, He is the Wisest of the wise.

Had they gone forth with you, they would not have increased you except in confusion, and they would have been active among you, seeking [to cause] you fitnah. And among you are avid listeners to them. And Allah is Knowing of the wrongdoers. (9:47)

لَوْ خَرَجُواْ فِيكُم مَّا زَادُوكُمْ إِلَّا خَبَالًا وَلَأَوْضَعُواْ خِلَالَكُمْ يَبْغُونَكُمُ ٱلْفِتْنَةَ وَفِيكُمْ سَمَّٰعُونَ لَهُمْۗ وَٱللَّهُ عَلِيمٌۢ بِٱلظَّٰلِمِينَ ۝

The texts of the revelation bore down heavily on them so they found them abhorrent, and being unable to carry them, they renounced them. They were unable to preserve the Sunnah so they ignored it. They found the texts of the Book and Sunnah combating their desires so they laid down laws and principles by which they could reject them or weaken them. Allah has unveiled their secrets and propounded parables for them. Know that each generation that succeeds them is like them and so He has described them for His friends that they may be aware of them. He says:

That is because they disliked what Allah revealed, so He rendered worthless their deeds. (47:9)

ذَٰلِكَ بِأَنَّهُمْ كَرِهُوا۟ مَآ أَنزَلَ ٱللَّهُ فَأَحْبَطَ أَعْمَٰلَهُمْ ۝

What is [the matter] with you [that you are] two groups concerning the hypocrites, while Allah has made them fall back [into error and disbelief] for what they earned.

Do you wish to guide those whom Allah has sent astray? And he whom Allah sends astray - never will you find for him a way [of guidance]. (4:88)

۞ فَمَا لَكُمْ فِى ٱلْمُنَٰفِقِينَ فِئَتَيْنِ وَٱللَّهُ أَرْكَسَهُم بِمَا كَسَبُوٓا۟ أَتُرِيدُونَ أَن تَهْدُوا۟ مَنْ أَضَلَّ ٱللَّهُ وَمَن يُضْلِلِ ٱللَّهُ فَلَن تَجِدَ لَهُۥ سَبِيلًا ۝

This holds true for all who find the texts burdensome and see them coming between him and his innovations and desires; it seems to him that he has come across an unbreakable solid structure, so he trades them for false rhetoric; exchanging reality for illusion. This leading to the corruption of his inner and outer.

That is because they said to those who disliked what Allah sent down, "We will obey you in part of the matter." And Allah knows what they conceal. (47:26-28)

$$ذَٰلِكَ بِأَنَّهُمْ قَالُوا۟ لِلَّذِينَ كَرِهُوا۟ مَا نَزَّلَ ٱللَّهُ سَنُطِيعُكُمْ فِى بَعْضِ ٱلْأَمْرِ ۖ وَٱللَّهُ يَعْلَمُ إِسْرَارَهُمْ ﴿٢٦﴾$$

Then how [will it be] when the angels take them in death, striking their faces and their backs?

$$فَكَيْفَ إِذَا تَوَفَّتْهُمُ ٱلْمَلَـٰٓئِكَةُ يَضْرِبُونَ وُجُوهَهُمْ وَأَدْبَـٰرَهُمْ ﴿٢٧﴾$$

That is because they followed what angered Allah and disliked [what earns] His pleasure, so He rendered worthless their deeds.

$$ذَٰلِكَ بِأَنَّهُمُ ٱتَّبَعُوا۟ مَآ أَسْخَطَ ٱللَّهَ وَكَرِهُوا۟ رِضْوَٰنَهُۥ فَأَحْبَطَ أَعْمَـٰلَهُمْ ﴿٢٨﴾$$

They think that if they hide their disbelief and display their faith they will have acquired a great profit; but how can this be so when the All Seeing has unveiled their secrets?

Or do those in whose hearts is disease think that Allah would never expose their [feelings of] hatred? (47:29-30)

$$\text{أَمْ حَسِبَ ٱلَّذِينَ فِى قُلُوبِهِم مَّرَضٌ أَن لَّن يُخْرِجَ ٱللَّهُ أَضْغَٰنَهُمْ ۝}$$

And if We willed, We could show them to you, and you would know them by their mark; but you will surely know them by the tone of [their] speech. And Allah knows your deeds.

$$\text{وَلَوْ نَشَآءُ لَأَرَيْنَٰكَهُمْ فَلَعَرَفْتَهُم بِسِيمَٰهُمْ ۚ وَلَتَعْرِفَنَّهُمْ فِى لَحْنِ ٱلْقَوْلِ ۚ وَٱللَّهُ يَعْلَمُ أَعْمَٰلَكُمْ ۝}$$

How will they be when they are gathered on the Day of at-Talaq, and Allah, Mighty and Magnificent, manifests Himself and uncovers His shin? The Day when they are called to prostrate but are unable.

Their eyes humbled, humiliation will cover them. And they used to be invited to prostration while they were sound. (68:43)

خَٰشِعَةً أَبْصَٰرُهُمْ تَرْهَقُهُمْ ذِلَّةٌ ۖ وَقَدْ كَانُوا۟ يُدْعَوْنَ إِلَى ٱلسُّجُودِ وَهُمْ سَٰلِمُونَ ﴿٤٣﴾

How will they be when they are gathered together to traverse the Bridge spanning Hell? A bridge finer than a blade of hair and sharper than the edge of a sword, easy to slip off, entrenched in darkness and none can cross it save those guided by a light that shows them where to place their feet. Light is apportioned amongst man; the intensity of light each person has governs the swiftness by which he will cross that bridge. They are given a superficial light with which they accompany the Muslims, just as they used to accompany the Muslims in this life: outwardly praying, giving wealth-tax, performing the pilgrimage, & fasting. When they reach the middle of the bridge their light is blown out by the sharp wind of hypocrisy and they come to a halt in utter confusion, not knowing how to proceed. A wall containing a door is placed between them and the believers, the believers' side of which contains mercy, while the side upon which they find themselves in contains punishment. They cry out to the believers, who in the distance sparkle like stars.

On the [same] Day the hypocrite men and hypocrite women will say to those who believed, "Wait for us that we may acquire some of your light." It will be said, "Go back behind you and seek light." And a wall will be placed between them with a door, its interior containing mercy, but on the outside of it is torment. (57:13)

$$\text{يَوْمَ يَقُولُ ٱلْمُنَٰفِقُونَ وَٱلْمُنَٰفِقَٰتُ لِلَّذِينَ ءَامَنُوا۟ ٱنظُرُونَا نَقْتَبِسْ مِن نُّورِكُمْ قِيلَ ٱرْجِعُوا۟ وَرَآءَكُمْ فَٱلْتَمِسُوا۟ نُورًا فَضُرِبَ بَيْنَهُم بِسُورٍ لَّهُۥ بَابٌۢ بَاطِنُهُۥ فِيهِ ٱلرَّحْمَةُ وَظَٰهِرُهُۥ مِن قِبَلِهِ ٱلْعَذَابُ ﴿١٣﴾}$$

The hypocrites will call to the believers, "Were we not with you?" They will say, "Yes, but you afflicted yourselves and awaited [misfortune for us] and doubted, and wishful thinking deluded you until there came the command of Allah. And the Deceiver deceived you concerning Allah. (57:14-15)

$$\text{يُنَادُونَهُمْ أَلَمْ نَكُن مَّعَكُمْ قَالُوا۟ بَلَىٰ وَلَٰكِنَّكُمْ فَتَنتُمْ أَنفُسَكُمْ وَتَرَبَّصْتُمْ وَٱرْتَبْتُمْ وَغَرَّتْكُمُ ٱلْأَمَانِىُّ حَتَّىٰ جَآءَ أَمْرُ ٱللَّهِ وَغَرَّكُم بِٱللَّهِ ٱلْغَرُورُ ﴿١٤﴾}$$

So today no ransom will be taken from you or from those who disbelieved. Your refuge is the Fire. It is most worthy of you, and wretched is the destination.

$$\text{فَٱلۡيَوۡمَ لَا يُؤۡخَذُ مِنكُمۡ فِدۡيَةٌ وَلَا مِنَ ٱلَّذِينَ كَفَرُوٓاْۚ مَأۡوَىٰكُمُ ٱلنَّارُۖ هِيَ مَوۡلَىٰكُمۡۖ وَبِئۡسَ ٱلۡمَصِيرُ ۝}$$

We fasted with you, prayed with you, recited the Quean with you, and performed the pilgrimage with you; why have we been separated from you! They will reply, your bodies were with us but your hearts were with every deviant and every disbelieving tyrant.

The descriptions of these people are numerous; by Allah what we have omitted is more than we have mentioned. One could almost say that the whole Quran is about them due to their plenitude on the face of this earth and in its belly, namely their graves. There is not a single place on earth except that they are to be found therein. Hudhayfah once heard a person saying: O'Allah, destroy the hypocrites! He said: 'Son of my brother, were He to destroy the hypocrites you would find yourself walking down roads alone; because hardly anybody would be left!'

By Allah, the hearts of the Righteous Predecessors lived in dread of hypocrisy because they knew its major and minor manifestations, they knew is generalities and its details and they thought little of themselves to the point that they feared being one of the hypocrites. Umar Al-Khanab said to Hudhayfah, I ask you by Allah, did the Messenger of Allah (peace be upon him) count me as one of them? He replied, No, and I will not answer this question for any other after you. Ibn Abi Mulaykah said: I met 30 Companions of the Prophet, and found all of them fearing hypocrisy, and not one of them said that his faith was like the faith of Jibril and Mikail. None feels safe from hypocrisy but a hypocrite. One of the Companions supplicated thus, Allah, I take refuge with you from hypocritical submissiveness; When asked what it was he replied, that the body be seen to be submissive but the heart is not. By Allah, their hearts were overflowing with faith and certainty yet their fear of hypocrisy was great.

The faith of many people does not even begin to compare to theirs, yet they claim that their faith is like that of Jibril and Mikail!

The plant of hypocrisy grows from two stems: lying and ostentation. It grows out of two sources: weakness of spiritual insight and weakness of resolution. When these four factors exist, the plant of hypocrisy flourishes and grows firm. However, it grows by the side of waters on the brink of a crumbling precipice, so when they see the flood of reality on the Day when all secrets are disclosed, and the graves are emptied out, and the heart s contents are brought to light, the one whose capital was hypocrisy will discover that all he attained was a mirage.

But those who disbelieved - their deeds are like a mirage in a lowland which a thirsty one thinks is water until, when he comes to it, he finds it is nothing but finds Allah before Him, and He will pay him in full his due; and Allah is swift in account. (24: 39)

وَٱلَّذِينَ كَفَرُوٓاْ أَعْمَٰلُهُمْ كَسَرَابٍۭ بِقِيعَةٍ يَحْسَبُهُ ٱلظَّمْـَٔانُ مَآءً حَتَّىٰٓ إِذَا جَآءَهُۥ لَمْ يَجِدْهُ شَيْـًٔا وَوَجَدَ ٱللَّهَ عِندَهُۥ فَوَفَّىٰهُ حِسَابَهُۥ ۗ وَٱللَّهُ سَرِيعُ ٱلْحِسَابِ ۝

Their hearts are heedless of doing good but their bodies outwardly do so, and indecent deeds are frequently performed by them. When they hear the truth their hearts are too hard to accept it, but when they witness falsehood and hear fallacy, their hearts openly accept it and they lend a willing ear.

By Allah, these are the signs of hypocrisy, so beware of them! Beware of them before the judgment comes upon you: when they are entrusted with something they break the trust, when they promise they break it, when they speak they are not fair and just, when they are called to obedience they falter, when they are called to what Allah has revealed and to His Messenger they turn away, but when it suits their whims and desires they rush to it. Leave them to the subjugation and misery that they have chosen for themselves, and rely not on their contracts and trust not in their promises for they are liars.

And among them are those who made a covenant with Allah, [saying], "If He should give us from His bounty, we will surely spend in charity, and we will surely be among the righteous. (9:75-77

۞ وَمِنْهُم مَّنْ عَـٰهَدَ ٱللَّهَ لَئِنْ ءَاتَىٰنَا مِن فَضْلِهِۦ لَنَصَّدَّقَنَّ وَلَنَكُونَنَّ مِنَ ٱلصَّـٰلِحِينَ ﴿٧٥﴾

But when he gave them from His bounty, they were stingy with it and turned away while they refused.

فَلَمَّآ ءَاتَىٰهُم مِّن فَضْلِهِۦ بَخِلُوا۟ بِهِۦ وَتَوَلَّوا۟ وَّهُم مُّعْرِضُونَ ﴿٧٦﴾

So He penalized them with hypocrisy in their hearts until the Day they will meet Him - because they failed Allah in what they promised Him and because they [habitually] used to lie.

فَأَعْقَبَهُمْ نِفَاقًا فِى قُلُوبِهِمْ إِلَىٰ يَوْمِ يَلْقَوْنَهُۥ بِمَآ أَخْلَفُوا۟ ٱللَّهَ مَا وَعَدُوهُ وَبِمَا كَانُوا۟ يَكْذِبُونَ ﴿٧٧﴾

Allah said in Surah Al-Baqarah about the hypocrites: Those are the ones who have purchased error [in exchange] for guidance, so their transaction has brought no profit, nor were they guided. (2:16-20)

أُو۟لَٰٓئِكَ ٱلَّذِينَ ٱشْتَرَوُا۟ ٱلضَّلَٰلَةَ بِٱلْهُدَىٰ فَمَا رَبِحَت تِّجَٰرَتُهُمْ وَمَا كَانُوا۟ مُهْتَدِينَ ۝

Their example is that of one who kindled a fire, but when it illuminated what was around him, Allah took away their light and left them in darkness [so] they could not see.

مَثَلُهُمْ كَمَثَلِ ٱلَّذِى ٱسْتَوْقَدَ نَارًا فَلَمَّآ أَضَآءَتْ مَا حَوْلَهُۥ ذَهَبَ ٱللَّهُ بِنُورِهِمْ وَتَرَكَهُمْ فِى ظُلُمَٰتٍ لَّا يُبْصِرُونَ ۝

Deaf, dumb and blind - so they will not return [to the right path].

صُمٌّۢ بُكْمٌ عُمْىٌ فَهُمْ لَا يَرْجِعُونَ ۝

Or [it is] like a rainstorm from the sky within which is darkness, thunder and lightning. They put their fingers into their ears from the thunderclaps in dread of death. But Allah is encompassing of the disbelievers.

أَوْ كَصَيِّبٍ مِّنَ ٱلسَّمَآءِ فِيهِ ظُلُمَٰتٌ وَرَعْدٌ وَبَرْقٌ يَجْعَلُونَ أَصَٰبِعَهُمْ فِىٓ ءَاذَانِهِم مِّنَ ٱلصَّوَٰعِقِ حَذَرَ ٱلْمَوْتِۚ وَٱللَّهُ مُحِيطٌۢ بِٱلْكَٰفِرِينَ ﴿١٩﴾

The lightning almost snatches away their sight. Every time it lights [the way] for them, they walk therein; but when darkness comes over them, they stand [still]. And if Allah had willed, He could have taken away their hearing and their sight. Indeed, Allah is over all things competent.

يَكَادُ ٱلْبَرْقُ يَخْطَفُ أَبْصَٰرَهُمْ كُلَّمَآ أَضَآءَ لَهُم مَّشَوْا۟ فِيهِ وَإِذَآ أَظْلَمَ عَلَيْهِمْ قَامُوا۟ وَلَوْ شَآءَ ٱللَّهُ لَذَهَبَ بِسَمْعِهِمْ وَأَبْصَٰرِهِمْ إِنَّ ٱللَّهَ عَلَىٰ كُلِّ شَىْءٍ قَدِيرٌ ۝

Allah has propounded a parable for His enemies, the hypocrites, with a people who ignited a fire in order to acquire light and benefit-for they were a people on a journey who had lost their way. When this fire had alighted and lit up their surroundings, they were able to see the right path, they were able to see what would benefit them and what would harm them; but then, suddenly, the light was extinguished and they were left in darkness: all three routes to guidance were barred them. Deaf, dumb and blind, guidance comes to a servant from three doors: what he hears with his ears; what he sees with his eyes; and what he understands with his heart; these people s hearts are unable to comprehend, they cannot see, and neither can they hear.

It is also said that because they gained no benefit from their ears, sight, and hearts; they were as good as those who had no faculty of hearing, seeing, and comprehension; and hence were described as such. Both these opinions are of the same meaning and go hand-in-hand. They wzll not return, in the light they had seen the path of guidance, but when the light left them, they did not return to that guidance.

Allah said: '*Allah removed their light,*' placing the particle '*ba*' before the word '*light*', and there is a notable reason for this. That is that this usage serves to show that Allah has removed from them His special closeness that is reserved for the

86

believers only. Therefore, after His re- moving their light, He neither stays close to them or with them. They have no place in His sayings:

If you do not aid the Prophet - Allah has already aided him when those who disbelieved had driven him out [of Makkah] as one of two, when they were in the cave and he said to his companion, "Do not grieve; indeed Allah is with us." And Allah sent down his tranquility upon him and supported him with angels you did not see and made the word of those who disbelieved the lowest, while the word of Allah - that is the highest. And Allah is Exalted in Might and Wise. (9:40)

إِلَّا تَنصُرُوهُ فَقَدْ نَصَرَهُ ٱللَّهُ إِذْ أَخْرَجَهُ ٱلَّذِينَ كَفَرُوا۟ ثَانِيَ ٱثْنَيْنِ إِذْ هُمَا فِى ٱلْغَارِ إِذْ يَقُولُ لِصَٰحِبِهِۦ لَا تَحْزَنْ إِنَّ ٱللَّهَ مَعَنَا ۖ فَأَنزَلَ ٱللَّهُ سَكِينَتَهُۥ عَلَيْهِ وَأَيَّدَهُۥ بِجُنُودٍ لَّمْ تَرَوْهَا وَجَعَلَ كَلِمَةَ ٱلَّذِينَ كَفَرُوا۟ ٱلسُّفْلَىٰ ۗ وَكَلِمَةُ ٱللَّهِ هِىَ ٱلْعُلْيَا ۗ وَٱللَّهُ عَزِيزٌ حَكِيمٌ ﴿٤٠﴾

[Moses] said, "No! Indeed, with me is my Lord; He will guide me." (26:62)

قَالَ كَلَّا ۖ إِنَّ مَعِىَ رَبِّى سَيَهْدِينِ ﴿٦٢﴾

The example of those who disbelieve is like that of one who shouts at what hears nothing but calls and cries cattle or sheep - deaf, dumb and blind, so they do not understand. (2:171)

وَمَثَلُ ٱلَّذِينَ كَفَرُوا۟ كَمَثَلِ ٱلَّذِى يَنْعِقُ بِمَا لَا يَسْمَعُ إِلَّا دُعَآءً وَنِدَآءً صُمٌّ بُكْمٌ عُمْىٌ فَهُمْ لَا يَعْقِلُونَ ﴿١٧١﴾

Ponder carefully His saying, then when it had lit up all around them, how this light is clearly shown to be distinct and separate from them, for had it been a light that was intrinsic to them, it would not have left them.

Therefore it was a light that surrounded them but did not enter them, it was something fleeting whereas the darkness was something permanent and intrinsic to them. Hence the light returned to its source and the darkness remained in its source, all of this was done as a proof from Allah and for an all-encompassing wisdom that none but those endowed with understanding can see.

Ponder carefully His saying, Allah removed their light, how He did not say, Allah removed their fire, such that the wording would conform to that found at the beginning of this verse. Why is this? Fire has both the property to give light and the property to burn, so its property of light was removed leaving only the property to burn and harm.

Ponder carefully His saying their light how He did not say their glow, despite the fact that He said, then when it had lit up all around them. His religion which Allah has called light; His guidance which Allah has called light; one of His Names is the Light; and the prayer which is light. Allah s taking away their light means that He took all this away from them. Those who have purchased error [in exchange] for guidance, so their transaction has brought no profit, nor were they guided. (2:16)

أُولَٰئِكَ ٱلَّذِينَ ٱشْتَرَوُا۟ ٱلضَّلَٰلَةَ بِٱلْهُدَىٰ فَمَا رَبِحَت تِّجَٰرَتُهُمْ وَمَا كَانُوا۟ مُهْتَدِينَ ﴿١٦﴾

How they acquired this misguidance at the expense of guidance, giving it away happily. Hence they have sold light and guidance and bought darkness and misguidance, what a wretched transaction!

Ponder carefully how Allah says: Allah removed their light, but says: and left them in darkness, Allah said light in the singular and darkness in the plural. The truth is one, and that is Allah s Straight Path: the only path that leads to Him: worship- ping Allah Alone in accordance to what has been legislated upon the tongue of His Messenger (peace be upon him); not with one's own desires and innovations. However the ways of falsehood are many and this is why Allah mentions the truth in its singular form but falsehood in its plural.

Allah is the ally of those who believe. He brings them out from darkness into the light. And those who disbelieve - their allies are Taghut. They take them out of the light into darkness. Those are the companions of the Fire; they will abide eternally therein. (2:257)

$$\text{اللَّهُ وَلِيُّ الَّذِينَ ءَامَنُوا يُخْرِجُهُم مِّنَ الظُّلُمَاتِ إِلَى النُّورِ وَالَّذِينَ كَفَرُوا أَوْلِيَاؤُهُمُ الطَّاغُوتُ يُخْرِجُونَهُم مِّنَ النُّورِ إِلَى الظُّلُمَاتِ أُوْلَٰٓئِكَ أَصْحَابُ النَّارِ هُمْ فِيهَا خَالِدُونَ ۝}$$

And, [moreover], this is My path, which is straight, so follow it; and do not follow [other] ways, for you will be separated from His way. This has He instructed you that you may become righteous. (6:153)

وَأَنَّ هَٰذَا صِرَٰطِى مُسْتَقِيمًا فَٱتَّبِعُوهُ ۖ وَلَا تَتَّبِعُوا۟ ٱلسُّبُلَ فَتَفَرَّقَ بِكُمْ عَن سَبِيلِهِۦ ۚ ذَٰلِكُمْ وَصَّىٰكُم بِهِۦ لَعَلَّكُمْ تَتَّقُونَ ﴿١٥٣﴾

This does not contradict His saying, by which Allah guides those who pursue His pleasure to the ways of peace and brings them out from darkness into the light, by His permission, and guides them to a straight path. (5:16)

يَهْدِى بِهِ ٱللَّهُ مَنِ ٱتَّبَعَ رِضْوَٰنَهُۥ سُبُلَ ٱلسَّلَٰمِ وَيُخْرِجُهُم مِّنَ ٱلظُّلُمَٰتِ إِلَى ٱلنُّورِ بِإِذْنِهِۦ وَيَهْدِيهِمْ إِلَىٰ صِرَٰطٍ مُّسْتَقِيمٍ ﴿١٦﴾

For this verse makes reference to the ways and routes that can be taken to please Him, all of which are contained within His one path, the Straight Path. It is authentically reported that the Prophet (peace be upon him) drew a straight line on the ground and said, This is the path of Allah, then he drew lines to the left and right of this line and said, These are the other paths, at the head of every path is a devil calling to it, then he recited the verse,

(And, [moreover], this is My path, which is straight, so follow it; and do not follow [other] ways, for you will be separated from His way. This has He instructed you that you may become righteous.6:153)

وَأَنَّ هَٰذَا صِرَٰطِى مُسْتَقِيمًا فَٱتَّبِعُوهُ وَلَا تَتَّبِعُوا۟ ٱلسُّبُلَ فَتَفَرَّقَ بِكُمْ عَن سَبِيلِهِۦ ۚ ذَٰلِكُمْ وَصَّىٰكُم بِهِۦ لَعَلَّكُمْ تَتَّقُونَ ۝

It is also said in explanation to this first parable that it is a similitude for what the hypocrites kindle of the fire of trial and tribulation that they seek to covertly spread amongst the

Muslims, as such it would be in the same vein as His saying,

And the Jews say, "The hand of Allah is chained." Chained are their hands, and cursed are they for what they say. Rather, both His hands are extended; He spends however He wills. And that which has been revealed to you from your Lord will surely increase many of them in transgression and disbelief. And We have cast among them animosity and hatred until the Day of Resurrection. Every time they kindled the fire of war [against you], Allah extinguished it. And they strive throughout the land [causing] corruption, and Allah does not like corrupters. (5:64)

وَقَالَتِ ٱلْيَهُودُ يَدُ ٱللَّهِ مَغْلُولَةٌ غُلَّتْ أَيْدِيهِمْ وَلُعِنُوا۟ بِمَا قَالُوا۟ بَلْ يَدَاهُ مَبْسُوطَتَانِ يُنفِقُ كَيْفَ يَشَآءُ وَلَيَزِيدَنَّ كَثِيرًا مِّنْهُم مَّآ أُنزِلَ إِلَيْكَ مِن رَّبِّكَ طُغْيَٰنًا وَكُفْرًا وَأَلْقَيْنَا بَيْنَهُمُ ٱلْعَدَٰوَةَ وَٱلْبَغْضَآءَ إِلَىٰ يَوْمِ ٱلْقِيَٰمَةِ كُلَّمَآ أَوْقَدُوا۟ نَارًا لِّلْحَرْبِ أَطْفَأَهَا ٱللَّهُ وَيَسْعَوْنَ فِى ٱلْأَرْضِ فَسَادًا وَٱللَّهُ لَا يُحِبُّ ٱلْمُفْسِدِينَ ﴿٦٤﴾

So, Allah removed their light would have the same meaning as, Allah extinguishes it; the foiling of their efforts and the falsification of their claims would have the same meaning as leaving them in darkness and confusion: deaf, dumb, and blind.

It is very problematic that this latter explanation be the correct critical to this verse, even though it, in and of itself is true. The one who kindles the fire of war does not have light that surrounds him, and has no light that could be taken from him. The fact that they have been left in darkness, unable to see, means that they moved from a state in which they could see knowledge and guidance to a state of doubt and disbelief, not that they kindled the fire of war.

Al-Hasan said (RA): this refers to the hypocrite: he saw, then became blind; he knew, then rejected. This is why He says: they will not return, i.e., they will not return to the light that they left. Allah says with regards the disbelievers.

The example of those who disbelieve is like that of one who shouts at what hears nothing but calls and cries cattle or sheep - deaf, dumb and blind, so they do not understand. (2:17)

$$\text{وَمَثَلُ ٱلَّذِينَ كَفَرُوا۟ كَمَثَلِ ٱلَّذِى يَنْعِقُ بِمَا لَا يَسْمَعُ إِلَّا دُعَآءً وَنِدَآءً ۚ صُمٌّۢ بُكْمٌ عُمْىٌ فَهُمْ لَا يَعْقِلُونَ ﴿١٧١﴾}$$

and thereby negated comprehension from them as they are not people of faith and insight, not having entered Islam; But about the hypocrites, He negated the fact that they would return because they had believed, then disbelieved, and would not return to faith.

Then after propounding this parable of fire, Allah (SWT) propounds another parable for the hypocrites, this time of water.

Sayyib mentioned in the verse refers to driving rain which pours down from the sky. Here the guidance has been likened to water because guidance gives life to the hearts as water gives life to the earth and its trees.

The portion that the hypocrite gets from this guidance is the same as one who is caught in this storm-cloud but gets nothing from it.

They have no notion of its many benefits such as life for the earth, its animals, trees, and the vegetation that springs forth after rain. The darkness, thunder, and lightning in a storm cloud are not matters that are desired in and of themselves, rather they are matters that lead to the accomplishment of what is desired from this cloud.

The hypocrites suffices with merely seeing the outward effects of this cloud: the darkness, the thunder, the lightning, the cold, and the fact that he is prevented from travelling; but has no clue of the huge benefit that comes as a result of the beautiful rain. This is true of every short-sighted, dull witted human; his perception does not go deeper than seeing the outward form of things, like a beautiful woman, and he does not want to know what is behind and inside them. This is the state of the majority of creation except for a few amongst them. When the short-sighted only sees the hardship and toil that is to be found in Jihad, when he sees the fact that he could be killed, wounded, censured by certain people, he does not go forth for Jihad.

He is unable to probe deeper and realize the great benefits, the praiseworthy goals, and great rewards it contains.

When one of them desires to perform the pilgrimage to Makka but sees only the hardships entailed in the journey, the leaving of the comfort of his family, and the difficulties to be faced, he cannot see beyond this to what lies at the end of this beautiful journey and as such falters and does not undertake it. This is the state of hypocrites, those who lack spiritual insight and are weak of faith: those who try to find threats in the Quran, and complains that is too heavy, and only pursues their desire and lusts.

These ordinances wean the soul of its base qualities. Weaning is truly difficult for the child; and all men are children due to their intellects with the exception of those who have weaned and regulated them, and as such have comprehended the truth by way of knowledge and action. It is such people who are able to see what is behind this storm-cloud; what is behind the darkness, thunder, and lightning; it is such people who realize that this storm-cloud is the source of life for existence.

Islam has been likened to the cloud, because hearts are given life by it as the earth is by water; disbelief has been likened to darkness threat and promise to thunder and lightning. And trials and tribulations have been likened to thunder-bolts.

Both these parables contain great points of wisdom:

i) The one who is seeking light is seeking light from something else, not from himself; when that light goes, he remains in that original darkness. This is the state of the hypocrite; he affirms belief on his tongue but does not believe or have love in his heart; as such what light he acquires as a result of this is borrowed.

ii) Fire requires fuel to keep it alight. This fuel is comparable to food that is required to sustain animal life. Likewise the light of faith requires fuel so as to maintain it: beneficial knowledge and righteous action. If this fuel is taken away, it dies out.

iii) Darkness is of two types: a perpetual darkness which is not preceded by light and a temporal darkness which is pre- ceded by light. It is the latter of these two which is most severe upon the one who faces it. The darkness of the disbelievers is of the first type for they have never seen the light, the darkness of the hypocrites is of the second type for they saw the light and then were plunged in darkness.

iv) This parable points to their state in the Hereafter for there they will be given a superficial light just as their light in this world was superficial.

Then at the time when they need light most, it will suddenly die: they will halt on the Bridge and be unable to cross it for only those with firm light may do so. That light is only made firm with beneficial knowledge and righteous actions. Therefore their parable which describes their state in this life corresponds to their state in the Hereafter: when light is apportioned to the people before the Bridge, the light of the believers will remain and the light of the hypocrites will die. When this is understood one understands why Allah said, Allah removed their light.

For further detail one can read the hadith recorded by Muslim on the authority of Jabir bin Abdullah. He was asked about the crossing of the Bridge to which he replied, We would come on the Day of Judgment on a hill standing above the people. Then the people will be summoned along with the idols that they used to worship, one after another. Then our Lord, Blessed and Exalted, would come to us and say, Who are you waiting for? They would say, We are waiting for our Lord. He would say, I am your Lord. They say, We are not sure until we look upon You. He would then manifest Himself and laugh, and would leave with them following. Every person among them, the believer and hypocrite, would be given light. On the Bridge spanning Hell there would be hooks and spikes which would take whoever Allah willed.

Then the light of the hypocrites would die out and the believers would secure salvation. The first group saved would consist of seventy thousand people whose faces would be like the moon and they will not be judged.

The next group would have faces like the stars of the sky, and so on. The intercession would commence till the point that there would come out of Hellfire the one who said, 'None has the right to be worshipped save Allah,' there was only in his heart a barley grain s worth of faith. They would be brought to the courtyard of Paradise and the inhabitants of Paradise would sprinkle water over them…, to the end of the hadith.

Ponder carefully his saying, "...and would leave with them following. Every person among them, the believer and hypocrite, would be given light...," and ponder carefully His saying, "Allah removed their light and left them in darkness, unable to see," and ponder their state when their light is extinguished and they are left in the pitch of darkness whereas the believers proceed on, following their Lord. Ponder his (peace be upon him) saying in the hadith concerning the intercession, "Every nation will follow the god that they used to worship, the polytheist will follow his god and the person of Tawhid will follow Allah." Ponder His saying, "The Day the shin will be uncovered and they are invited to prostration but the disbelievers will not be able." (68:42)

$$\text{يَوْمَ يُكْشَفُ عَن سَاقٍ وَيُدْعَوْنَ إِلَى ٱلسُّجُودِ فَلَا يَسْتَطِيعُونَ ﴿٤٢﴾}$$

He (peace and blessing be upon him) mentioned this verse in the hadith of intercession on this occasion talked about in the previous hadith and in the hadith he said, "...so He will uncover His shin," and thereby made clear that it was His shin that was being talked about in the verse. Ponder all of this and you will come to understand a secret from the secrets of Tawhid, understanding of the Quran, and how Allah deals with the people of Tawhid as compared to the people of shirk;

The first parable deals with them acquiring darkness which is a similitude for misguidance and confusion, the opposite of which is guidance. The second parable deals with their acquiring fear, the opposite of which is safety and security. The hypocrites are not guided and neither are they safe.

They who believe and do not mix their belief with injustice - those will have security, and they are [rightly] guided. (6:82)

ٱلَّذِينَ ءَامَنُواْ وَلَمْ يَلْبِسُوٓاْ إِيمَٰنَهُم بِظُلْمٍ أُوْلَٰٓئِكَ لَهُمُ ٱلْأَمْنُ وَهُم مُّهْتَدُونَ ﴿٨٢﴾

Ibn Abbas and other exegetes said, "The similitude of these people s hypocrisy is that of a person who kindled a fire in a dark night on a terrifying occasion. He warms himself up, sees what is around him, and is saved from what he feared; then while in that state, the fire is suddenly extinguished and he remains once again in that darkness in a state of fear and utter confusion. The hypocrites, by their outwardly testifying to faith, have secured their wealth and children, they marry the believers, they inherit from them, and they acquire a portion of the war booty. This is their light, but when they die, they return once again to darkness and fear."

The acquiring of light and its removal has been explained variously to take place in this life, or the life of the grave, or in the Hereafter. The correct position is that it occurs in all three stages of life, for they are recompensed for their state in this world in all three stages with.

Whoever does righteousness - it is for his [own] soul; and whoever does evil [does so] against it. And your

Lord is not ever unjust to [His] servants. (41:46)

$$\text{مَّنْ عَمِلَ صَالِحًا فَلِنَفْسِهِ ۖ وَمَنْ أَسَاءَ فَعَلَيْهَا ۗ وَمَا رَبُّكَ بِظَلَّامٍ لِّلْعَبِيدِ ﴿٤٦﴾}$$

In the resurrection a person shall reap what he sowed in this world and that is why it is called the Day of Recompense.

And whoever is blind in this [life] will be blind in the Hereafter and more astray in way. (17:72)

$$\text{وَمَن كَانَ فِي هَٰذِهِ أَعْمَىٰ فَهُوَ فِي الْآخِرَةِ أَعْمَىٰ وَأَضَلُّ سَبِيلًا ﴿٧٢﴾}$$

And Allah increases those who were guided, in guidance, and the enduring good deeds are better to your Lord for reward and better for recourse. (19:76)

$$وَيَزِيدُ اللَّهُ الَّذِينَ اهْتَدَوْا هُدًى ۗ وَالْبَاقِيَاتُ الصَّالِحَاتُ خَيْرٌ عِندَ رَبِّكَ ثَوَابًا وَخَيْرٌ مَّرَدًّا ۝$$

To return to the discussion at hand...Allah, the Blessed and Exalted, has propounded two parables, one for fire and one for water, in Surah Al-Baqarah, Surah ar-Ra'd, and Surah an-Nur. This is because life comes about through water and light; the believer has a living and illuminated heart, and the hypocrite has a dead and dark heart. Allah, Exalted is He says:

And is one who was dead and We gave him life and made for him light by which to walk among the people like one who is in darkness, never to emerge therefrom? Thus it has been made pleasing to the disbelievers that which they were doing. (6:122)

أَوَمَن كَانَ مَيْتًا فَأَحْيَيْنَاهُ وَجَعَلْنَا لَهُ نُورًا يَمْشِى بِهِ فِى ٱلنَّاسِ كَمَن مَّثَلُهُ فِى ٱلظُّلُمَاتِ لَيْسَ بِخَارِجٍ مِّنْهَا ۚ كَذَٰلِكَ زُيِّنَ لِلْكَافِرِينَ مَا كَانُوا۟ يَعْمَلُونَ ﴿١٢٢﴾

Not equal are the blind and the seeing. (35:19-22)

وَمَا يَسْتَوِى ٱلْأَعْمَىٰ وَٱلْبَصِيرُ ﴿١٩﴾

Nor are the darkness and the light.

وَلَا ٱلظُّلُمَاتُ وَلَا ٱلنُّورُ ﴿٢٠﴾

Nor are the shade and the heat.

وَلَا ٱلظِّلُّ وَلَا ٱلْحَرُورُ ﴿٢١﴾

And not equal are the living and the dead. Indeed, Allah causes to hear whom He wills, but you cannot make hear those in the graves.

$$\text{وَمَا يَسْتَوِي ٱلْأَحْيَاءُ وَلَا ٱلْأَمْوَاتُ ۚ إِنَّ ٱللَّهَ يُسْمِعُ مَن يَشَاءُ ۖ وَمَا أَنتَ بِمُسْمِعٍ مَّن فِي ٱلْقُبُورِ ﴿٢٢﴾}$$

Therefore He considered those who follow His guidance, and illuminate themselves with His light to be alive, taking refuge under a shade that saves them from the heat of doubts, misguidance, innovation, and shirk. He considered one who does not do so to be blind and dead, submerged in the heat of disbelief, shirk and misguidance, engulfed in layer after layer of darkness.

Allah, says in Surah al-Baqarah concerning the hypocrites:

Or [it is] like a rainstorm from the sky within which is darkness, thunder and lightning. They put their fingers in their ears against the thunderclaps in dread of death. But Allah is encompassing of the disbelievers. (2:19)

أَوْ كَصَيِّبٍ مِّنَ ٱلسَّمَآءِ فِيهِ ظُلُمَٰتٌ وَرَعْدٌ وَبَرْقٌ يَجْعَلُونَ أَصَٰبِعَهُمْ فِىٓ ءَاذَانِهِم مِّنَ ٱلصَّوَٰعِقِ حَذَرَ ٱلْمَوْتِ ۚ وَٱللَّهُ مُحِيطٌۢ بِٱلْكَٰفِرِينَ ﴿١٩﴾

The lightning almost snatches away their sight. Every time it lights [the way] for them, they walk therein; but when darkness comes over them, they stand [still]. And if Allah had willed, He could have taken away their hearing and their sight. Indeed, Allah is over all things competent. (2:20)

يَكَادُ ٱلۡبَرۡقُ يَخۡطَفُ أَبۡصَٰرَهُمۡۖ كُلَّمَآ أَضَآءَ لَهُم مَّشَوۡاْ فِيهِ وَإِذَآ أَظۡلَمَ عَلَيۡهِمۡ قَامُواْۚ وَلَوۡ شَآءَ ٱللَّهُ لَذَهَبَ بِسَمۡعِهِمۡ وَأَبۡصَٰرِهِمۡۚ إِنَّ ٱللَّهَ عَلَىٰ كُلِّ شَيۡءٍ قَدِيرٌ ۝

A storm-cloud in the sky, full of darkness, thunder and lightning. They thrust their fingers in their ears against the thunderclaps, fearful of death.

Allah encompasses the disbelievers. The lightning all but snatches away their sight. Whenever they have light, they walk therein but whenever darkness covers them, they halt. If Allah wished, He could take away their hearing and their sight; for Allah has power over all things.

The saying of the Exalted, a storm-cloud, Sayyib means rain. Allah has set forth a parable in this verse for the guidance and knowledge that the Messenger of Allah (peace be upon him) came with, likening it to rain. It is likened so because knowledge and guidance is a source of life for the souls just as water is a source of life for the bodies. This aspect of the parable was indicated by Allah in His saying,

Allah knows best. And it is He who sends the winds as good tidings before His mercy until, when they have carried heavy rainclouds, We drive them to a dead land and We send down rain therein and bring forth thereby [some] of all the fruits. Thus will We bring forth the dead; perhaps you may be reminded. (7:57-58)

وَهُوَ ٱلَّذِى يُرْسِلُ ٱلرِّيَٰحَ بُشْرًۢا بَيْنَ يَدَىْ رَحْمَتِهِۦۖ حَتَّىٰٓ إِذَآ أَقَلَّتْ سَحَابًا ثِقَالًا سُقْنَٰهُ لِبَلَدٍ مَّيِّتٍ فَأَنزَلْنَا بِهِ ٱلْمَآءَ فَأَخْرَجْنَا بِهِۦ مِن كُلِّ ٱلثَّمَرَٰتِۚ كَذَٰلِكَ نُخْرِجُ ٱلْمَوْتَىٰ لَعَلَّكُمْ تَذَكَّرُونَ ۝٥٧

And the good land - its vegetation emerges by permission of its Lord; but that which is bad - nothing emerges except sparsely, with difficulty. Thus do We diversify the signs for a people who are grateful.

وَٱلْبَلَدُ ٱلطَّيِّبُ يَخْرُجُ نَبَاتُهُۥ بِإِذْنِ رَبِّهِۦۖ وَٱلَّذِى خَبُثَ لَا يَخْرُجُ إِلَّا نَكِدًاۚ كَذَٰلِكَ نُصَرِّفُ ٱلْءَايَٰتِ لِقَوْمٍ يَشْكُرُونَ ۝٥٨

The Messenger (peace be upon him) explained this aspect of the parable wherein he (peace be upon him) said: The similitude of the guidance and knowledge that Allah has sent me with is like abundant rain falling on the earth; some of which has fertile soil that absorbed the rain water and brought forth vegetation and grass in abundance; and another portion of it was hard and held the rain water and Allah benefited the people with it and they utilized it for drinking, making their animals drink from it, and for irrigation of the land for cultivation; and a portion of it was barren which could neither hold water nor bring forth vegetation. This similitude betokens the one who understands the religion, benefits from what Allah has sent me with, learns and teaches it; and the one who pays not heed and does not accept the guidance with which I have been sent.

Full of darkness, Allah has set forth a parable in this verse regarding the doubts and suspicion that have afflicted the hypocrites with respect to the Quran-comparing these to the dark ness in the storm-cloud which in turn has been set forth as a similitude to the Quran. Allah has illustrated a number of occasions, in other verses, which are like darkness for them because they increase them only in blindness. He says:

And thus we have made you a just community that you will be witnesses over the people and the Messenger will be a witness over you. And We did not make the Qiblah which you used to face except that We might make evident who would follow the Messenger from who would turn back on his heels. And indeed, it is difficult except for those whom Allah has guided.

And never would Allah have caused you to lose your faith. Indeed Allah is, to the people, Kind and Merciful. (2:143)

وَكَذَٰلِكَ جَعَلْنَٰكُمْ أُمَّةً وَسَطًا لِّتَكُونُوا۟ شُهَدَآءَ عَلَى ٱلنَّاسِ وَيَكُونَ ٱلرَّسُولُ عَلَيْكُمْ شَهِيدًا ۗ وَمَا جَعَلْنَا ٱلْقِبْلَةَ ٱلَّتِى كُنتَ عَلَيْهَآ إِلَّا لِنَعْلَمَ مَن يَتَّبِعُ ٱلرَّسُولَ مِمَّن يَنقَلِبُ عَلَىٰ عَقِبَيْهِ ۚ وَإِن كَانَتْ لَكَبِيرَةً إِلَّا عَلَى ٱلَّذِينَ هَدَى ٱللَّهُ ۗ وَمَا كَانَ ٱللَّهُ لِيُضِيعَ إِيمَٰنَكُمْ ۚ إِنَّ ٱللَّهَ بِٱلنَّاسِ لَرَءُوفٌ رَّحِيمٌ ﴿١٤٣﴾

The abrogation of the Qiblah from Jerusalem to the Kabah made the people having weak conviction think that the Messenger (peace be upon him) was not certain of his message: for one day he was facing one direction in prayer and another day another direction! This is why Allah has said:

The foolish among the people will say, "What has turned them away from their qiblah, which they used to face?" Say, "To Allah belongs the east and the west. He guides whom He wills to a straight path." (2:142)

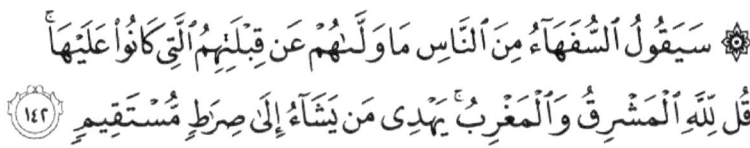

So Allah has made clear that the abrogation of the Qiblah was hard upon those whom Allah did not guide and strengthen his conviction in His saying, Indeed it was a great test except for those whom Allah guided.

Another example lies in His saying: And [remember, O Muhammad], when We told you, "Indeed, your Lord has encompassed the people."

And We did not make the sight which We showed you except as a trial for the people, as was the accursed tree [mentioned] in the Qur'an. And We threaten them, but it increases them not except in great transgression. (17:60)

وَإِذْ قُلْنَا لَكَ إِنَّ رَبَّكَ أَحَاطَ بِٱلنَّاسِ وَمَا جَعَلْنَا ٱلرُّءْيَا ٱلَّتِىٓ أَرَيْنَٰكَ إِلَّا فِتْنَةً لِّلنَّاسِ وَٱلشَّجَرَةَ ٱلْمَلْعُونَةَ فِى ٱلْقُرْءَانِ وَنُخَوِّفُهُمْ فَمَا يَزِيدُهُمْ إِلَّا طُغْيَٰنًا كَبِيرًا ۝

What he (peace be upon him) was shown on the night of Isra and Miraj was from amongst the miracles and wonders bestowed him, there- fore it was a means of strengthening the belief of the disbelievers that he (peace be upon him) was a liar because they thought that what he was informing them of could not possibly occur.

Hence, this event was a means by which the misguided increased in misguidance.

Likewise, the accursed tree in the Quran, which is the tree of Zaqqum, was also a means of increasing the misguided in misguidance, for when they heard the Prophet (peace be upon him) reciting,

Indeed, it is a tree issuing from the bottom of the Hellfire, (37:64)

$$\text{إِنَّهَا شَجَرَةٌ تَخْرُجُ فِي أَصْلِ الْجَحِيمِ ﴿٦٤﴾}$$

They said, His lie has become clear: a tree will not grow in a desert so how can one grow in the bottom of Hellfire!

Another example lies in His saying:

And We have not made the keepers of the Fire except angels. And We have not made their number except as a trial for those who disbelieve - that those who were given the Scripture will be convinced and those who have believed will increase in faith and those who were given the Scripture and the believers will not doubt and that those in whose hearts is hypocrisy and the disbelievers will say, "What does Allah intend by this as an example?" Thus does Allah leave astray whom He wills and guides whom He wills. And none knows the soldiers of your Lord except Him. And mention of the Fire is not but a reminder to humanity. (74:31)

وَمَا جَعَلْنَا أَصْحَابَ ٱلنَّارِ إِلَّا مَلَٰٓئِكَةً ۙ وَمَا جَعَلْنَا عِدَّتَهُمْ إِلَّا فِتْنَةً لِّلَّذِينَ كَفَرُوا۟ لِيَسْتَيْقِنَ ٱلَّذِينَ أُوتُوا۟ ٱلْكِتَٰبَ وَيَزْدَادَ ٱلَّذِينَ ءَامَنُوٓا۟ إِيمَٰنًا ۙ وَلَا يَرْتَابَ ٱلَّذِينَ أُوتُوا۟ ٱلْكِتَٰبَ وَٱلْمُؤْمِنُونَ ۙ وَلِيَقُولَ ٱلَّذِينَ فِى قُلُوبِهِم مَّرَضٌ وَٱلْكَٰفِرُونَ مَاذَآ أَرَادَ ٱللَّهُ بِهَٰذَا مَثَلًا ۚ كَذَٰلِكَ يُضِلُّ ٱللَّهُ مَن يَشَآءُ وَيَهْدِى مَن يَشَآءُ ۚ وَمَا يَعْلَمُ جُنُودَ رَبِّكَ إِلَّا هُوَ ۚ وَمَا هِىَ إِلَّا ذِكْرَىٰ لِلْبَشَرِ ﴿٣١﴾

When he (peace be upon him) recited the verse:

Over it are nineteen [angels]. (74:30)

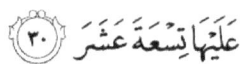

Some of the people said: This is such a small number guarding this Fire that Muhammad (peace be upon him) thinks that we shall enter that we are capable of killing them and then taking Paradise by force!

Allah, Exalted is He, did this as a test for them, and He has an all-encompassing wisdom behind doing so, and He is Exalted, far above what the unbelievers say.

'Thunder,' Allah has set forth a similitude to thunder due to what the Quean contains of rebukes that ring in the ears and stir the heart, some of which are mentioned in other verses such as His sayings: But if they turn away, then say, "I have warned you of a thunderbolt like the thunderbolt [that struck] 'Aad and Thamud. (41:13)

فَإِنْ أَعْرَضُوا فَقُلْ أَنذَرْتُكُمْ صَاعِقَةً مِّثْلَ صَاعِقَةِ عَادٍ وَثَمُودَ ﴿١٣﴾

O you who were given the Scripture, believe in what We have sent down [to Muhammad], confirming that which is with you, before We obliterate faces and turn them toward their backs or curse them as We cursed the sabbath-breakers. And ever is the decree of Allah accomplished. (4:47)

$$\text{يَٰٓأَيُّهَا ٱلَّذِينَ أُوتُوا۟ ٱلْكِتَٰبَ ءَامِنُوا۟ بِمَا نَزَّلْنَا مُصَدِّقًا لِّمَا مَعَكُم مِّن قَبْلِ أَن نَّطْمِسَ وُجُوهًا فَنَرُدَّهَا عَلَىٰٓ أَدْبَارِهَآ أَوْ نَلْعَنَهُمْ كَمَا لَعَنَّآ أَصْحَٰبَ ٱلسَّبْتِ ۚ وَكَانَ أَمْرُ ٱللَّهِ مَفْعُولًا ۝٤٧}$$

Say, "I only advise you of one [thing] - that you stand for Allah, [seeking truth] in pairs and individually, and then give thought." There is not in your companion any madness. He is only a warner to you before a severe punishment. (34:46)

بِسْمِ اللَّهِ ۞ قُلْ إِنَّمَا أَعِظُكُم بِوَاحِدَةٍ ۖ أَن تَقُومُوا۟ لِلَّهِ مَثْنَىٰ وَفُرَادَىٰ ثُمَّ تَتَفَكَّرُوا۟ ۚ مَا بِصَاحِبِكُم مِّن جِنَّةٍ ۚ إِنْ هُوَ إِلَّا نَذِيرٌ لَّكُم بَيْنَ يَدَىْ عَذَابٍ شَدِيدٍ ۝

Bukhari records in the chapter pertaining to the commentary of Surah at-Tur, on the authority of Jubayr ibn Mutim, who said, I heard the Messenger of Allah reciting Surah at-Tur in Maghrib prayer, and when he reached this verse: *'Were they created out of nothing, or were they themselves the creators? Or did they create the heavens and the earth? No, in truth, they have no certainty. Or do they possess the treasures of your Lord or do they have control of them?"* my heart felt like it was flying!

And other such rebukes and cataclysmic announcements from which the hypocrites were in continuous fear of, to the point that Allah said of them. And when you see them, their forms please you, and if they speak, you listen to their speech. [They are] as if they were pieces of wood propped up - they think that every shout is against them. They are the enemy, so beware of them. May Allah destroy them; how are they deluded? (63:4)

﴿وَإِذَا رَأَيْتَهُمْ تُعْجِبُكَ أَجْسَامُهُمْ وَإِن يَقُولُوا۟ تَسْمَعْ لِقَوْلِهِمْ كَأَنَّهُمْ خُشُبٌ مُّسَنَّدَةٌ يَحْسَبُونَ كُلَّ صَيْحَةٍ عَلَيْهِمْ هُمُ ٱلْعَدُوُّ فَٱحْذَرْهُمْ قَٰتَلَهُمُ ٱللَّهُ أَنَّىٰ يُؤْفَكُونَ﴾ (٤)

The verse that we are in the process of explaining, even if it is with regards to hypocrites, consideration is given to the generality of the wording and not to the specific reason for its revelation.

'and lightning,' Allah has set forth a similitude to lightning due to what the Quran contains of the light of decisive evidences and radiant proofs. It has been made clear that the Quran is a light by which Allah uncovers the darkness of ignorance, doubt, and shirk; in the same way that the natural light uncovers dark recesses. He says: O mankind, there has come to you a conclusive proof from your Lord, and We have sent down to you a clear light. (4:174)

$$\text{يَٰٓأَيُّهَا ٱلنَّاسُ قَدْ جَآءَكُم بُرْهَٰنٌ مِّن رَّبِّكُمْ وَأَنزَلْنَآ إِلَيْكُمْ نُورًا مُّبِينًا ۝}$$

And thus We have revealed to you an inspiration of Our command. You did not know what is the Book or [what is] faith, but We have made it a light by which We guide whom We will of Our servants. And indeed, [O

Muhammad], you guide to a straight path - (42:52)

وَكَذَٰلِكَ أَوْحَيْنَا إِلَيْكَ رُوحًا مِّنْ أَمْرِنَا ۚ مَا كُنتَ تَدْرِى مَا ٱلْكِتَٰبُ وَلَا ٱلْإِيمَٰنُ وَلَٰكِن جَعَلْنَٰهُ نُورًا نَّهْدِى بِهِۦ مَن نَّشَآءُ مِنْ عِبَادِنَا ۚ وَإِنَّكَ لَتَهْدِىٓ إِلَىٰ صِرَٰطٍ مُّسْتَقِيمٍ ۝

Those who follow the Messenger, the unlettered prophet, whom they find written in what they have of the Torah and the Gospel, who enjoins upon them what is right and forbids them what is wrong and makes lawful for them the good things and prohibits for them the evil and relieves them of their burden and the shackles which were upon them. So they who have believed in him, honored him, supported him and followed the light which was sent down with him - it is those who will be the successful. (7:157)

ٱلَّذِينَ يَتَّبِعُونَ ٱلرَّسُولَ ٱلنَّبِيَّ ٱلْأُمِّيَّ ٱلَّذِي يَجِدُونَهُۥ مَكْتُوبًا عِندَهُمْ فِي ٱلتَّوْرَىٰةِ وَٱلْإِنجِيلِ يَأْمُرُهُم بِٱلْمَعْرُوفِ وَيَنْهَىٰهُمْ عَنِ ٱلْمُنكَرِ وَيُحِلُّ لَهُمُ ٱلطَّيِّبَٰتِ وَيُحَرِّمُ عَلَيْهِمُ ٱلْخَبَٰٓئِثَ وَيَضَعُ عَنْهُمْ إِصْرَهُمْ وَٱلْأَغْلَٰلَ ٱلَّتِي كَانَتْ عَلَيْهِمْ ۚ فَٱلَّذِينَ ءَامَنُوا۟ بِهِۦ وَعَزَّرُوهُ وَنَصَرُوهُ وَٱتَّبَعُوا۟ ٱلنُّورَ ٱلَّذِيٓ أُنزِلَ مَعَهُۥٓ ۙ أُو۟لَٰٓئِكَ هُمُ ٱلْمُفْلِحُونَ ۝١٥٧

'Allah encompasses the disbelievers,' some of the scholars said, encompasses the disbelievers means destroys them, and this opinion is testified to by the saying of Allah: [Jacob] said, "Never will I send him with you until you give me a promise by Allah that you will bring him [back] to me, unless you should be surrounded by enemies." And when they had given their promise, he said, "Allah, over what we say, is Witness." (12:66)

قَالَ لَنْ أُرْسِلَهُۥ مَعَكُمْ حَتَّىٰ تُؤْتُونِ مَوْثِقًا مِّنَ ٱللَّهِ لَتَأْتُنَّنِي بِهِۦٓ إِلَّآ أَن يُحَاطَ بِكُمْ ۖ فَلَمَّآ ءَاتَوْهُ مَوْثِقَهُمْ قَالَ ٱللَّهُ عَلَىٰ مَا نَقُولُ وَكِيلٌ ﴿٦٦﴾

Meaning: unless an enemy destroys you to your last man. It is said that it means overcome and both opinions are close in meaning because the one who is destroyed is not destroyed until he is surrounded on all sides and their remains no way for him to escape to safety and the same applies to the one who is over- come. Also in this respect, understanding surrounded to mean destroyed is His sayings:

And his fruits were encompassed [by ruin], so he began to turn his hands about [in dismay] over what he had spent on it, while it had collapsed upon its trellises, and said, "Oh, I wish I had not associated with my Lord anyone." (18): 42]

وَأُحِيطَ بِثَمَرِهِ فَأَصْبَحَ يُقَلِّبُ كَفَّيْهِ عَلَىٰ مَا أَنفَقَ فِيهَا وَهِيَ خَاوِيَةٌ عَلَىٰ عُرُوشِهَا وَيَقُولُ يَٰلَيْتَنِي لَمْ أُشْرِكْ بِرَبِّي أَحَدًا ﴿٤٢﴾

It is He who enables you to travel on land and sea until, when you are in ships and they sail with them by a good wind and they rejoice therein, there comes a storm wind and the waves come upon them from everywhere and they assume that they are surrounded, supplicating Allah, sincere to Him in religion, "If You should save us from this, we will surely be among the thankful." (10:22)

هُوَ ٱلَّذِى يُسَيِّرُكُمْ فِى ٱلْبَرِّ وَٱلْبَحْرِ حَتَّىٰ إِذَا كُنتُمْ فِى ٱلْفُلْكِ وَجَرَيْنَ بِهِم بِرِيحٍ طَيِّبَةٍ وَفَرِحُوا۟ بِهَا جَآءَتْهَا رِيحٌ عَاصِفٌ وَجَآءَهُمُ ٱلْمَوْجُ مِن كُلِّ مَكَانٍ وَظَنُّوٓا۟ أَنَّهُمْ أُحِيطَ بِهِمْ دَعَوُا۟ ٱللَّهَ مُخْلِصِينَ لَهُ ٱلدِّينَ لَئِنْ أَنجَيْتَنَا مِنْ هَٰذِهِۦ لَنَكُونَنَّ مِنَ ٱلشَّٰكِرِينَ ﴿٢٢﴾

'The lightning all but snatches away their sight,' meaning that the light of the Quran blinds their eyes due to its extreme brilliance, in the same way that a flash of lightning almost snatches way the sight of the onlooker due to its extreme light. This is more so the case if the sight is weak because as the sight gets weaker, flashes of light affect it more severely. The poet said:

Like the day increases the sight of mortals Due to its light and blinds the eyes of the bats

Another said: The bats are blinded by the light of day, And the covering of the dark night agrees with them

The eyes of the disbelievers and the hypocrites are completely weak, and the severity of the dazzling lights of the Quran increases them in blindness. Allah has clarified this blindness with His sayings:

Then is he who knows that what has been revealed to you from your Lord is the truth like one who is blind? They will only be reminded who are people of understanding. (13:19)

﴿ أَفَمَن يَعْلَمُ أَنَّمَا أُنزِلَ إِلَيْكَ مِن رَّبِّكَ ٱلْحَقُّ كَمَنْ هُوَ أَعْمَىٰٓ إِنَّمَا يَتَذَكَّرُ أُو۟لُوا۟ ٱلْأَلْبَـٰبِ ﴾ ﴿١٩﴾

Not equal are the blind and the seeing, (35:19)

﴿ وَمَا يَسْتَوِى ٱلْأَعْمَىٰ وَٱلْبَصِيرُ ﴾ ﴿١٩﴾

Some of the scholar said that the verse: *'The lightning all but snatches away their sight,'* means that the clear and unequivocal verses of the Quran reveal the weaknesses and defects of the hypocrites.

'Whenever they have light, they walk therein but whenever dark- ness covers them, they halt,' Allah sets forth a similitude for the hypocrites in this verse that when the Quran agrees with their desires and expectations they act according to it, like the fa-vours they scrounge off the believers such as their inheriting from them, their receiving a share of the war booty, and their being secure from being killed despite the disbelief that is in their hearts. Whenever it does not agree with their desires such as their being commanded to expend their selves and wealth in Jihad they falter and

procrastinate. Allah has pointed this out in His saying:

And when they are called to [the words of] Allah and His Messenger to judge between them, at once a party of them turns aside [in refusal]. (24:48-49)

وَإِذَا دُعُوٓا۟ إِلَى ٱللَّهِ وَرَسُولِهِۦ لِيَحْكُمَ بَيْنَهُمْ إِذَا فَرِيقٌ مِّنْهُم مُّعْرِضُونَ ﴿٤٨﴾

But if the right is theirs, they come to him in prompt obedience.

وَإِن يَكُن لَّهُمُ ٱلْحَقُّ يَأْتُوٓا۟ إِلَيْهِ مُذْعِنِينَ ﴿٤٩﴾

Some of the scholars said that: '*Whenever they have light, they walk therein,*' means that whenever Allah favours them with wealth and well-being they say:

This religion is the truth, ever since we have held onto to it we have only acquired good. (but whenever darkness covers them, they halt means that when they come across poverty or illness, or they have daughters born to them rather than sons they say, This has not happened to us except due to the evil of this religion, and they apostate from it. This explanation is proven by the saying of Allah: And of the people is he who worships Allah on an edge. If he is touched by good, he is reassured by it; but if he is struck by trial, he turns on his face [to the other direction]. He has lost [this] world and the Hereafter. That is what is the manifest loss. (22:11)

وَمِنَ ٱلنَّاسِ مَن يَعْبُدُ ٱللَّهَ عَلَىٰ حَرْفٍۖ فَإِنْ أَصَابَهُۥ خَيْرٌ ٱطْمَأَنَّ بِهِۦۖ وَإِنْ أَصَابَتْهُ فِتْنَةٌ ٱنقَلَبَ عَلَىٰ وَجْهِهِۦ خَسِرَ ٱلدُّنْيَا وَٱلْأَخِرَةَۚ ذَٰلِكَ هُوَ ٱلْخُسْرَانُ ٱلْمُبِينُ ﴿١١﴾

Some of the scholars said: '*Its flashing for them*,' means their cognition of some of the truth and its darkness means the doubt that presents itself to them concerning Islam.

And Allah knows best.

Great Prayer:

When the persecution of Qurayish intensified following the death of his uncle and his wife, the Prophet (peace be upon him) went to the tribe of At-Taif, hoping that would listen to him and support him. But they rejected him and told their children to throw rocks at him until blood flowed to his body and feet. The Prophet (peace be upon him) sought refuge in one of the gardens of At-Taif, and then he said the following beautiful and humble prayer to Allah:

اَللّٰهُمَّ اِلَيْكَ اَشْكُو ضَعْفَ قُوَّتِي وَقِلَّةَ حِيلَتِي وَهَوَانِي عَلَى النَّاسِ يَاأَرْحَمَ الرَّاحِمِينَ أَنْتَ رَبُّ الْمُسْتَضْعَفِينَ وَأَنْتَ رَبِّي إِلَى مَنْ تَكِلُنِي إِلَى بَعِيدٍ يَتَجَهَّمُنِي أَمْ إِلَى عَدُوٍّ مَلَّكْتَهُ أَمْرِي إِنْ لَمْ يَكُنْ بِكَ عَلَيَّ غَضَبٌ فَلَا أُبَالِي وَلٰكِنَّ عَافِيَتَكَ هِيَ أَوْسَعُ لِي أَعُوذُ بِنُورِ وَجْهِكَ الَّذِي أَشْرَقَتْ لَهُ الظُّلُمَاتُ وَصَلَحَ عَلَيْهِ أَمْرُ الدُّنْيَا وَالْآخِرَةِ مِنْ أَنْ تُنْزِلَ بِي غَضَبَكَ أَوْ يَحِلَّ عَلَيَّ سَخَطُكَ لَكَ الْعُتْبَى حَتَّى تَرْضَى وَلَا حَوْلَ وَلَا قُوَّةَ إِلَّا بِكَ

"O'Allah, to You do I complain of my weakness, little resource and lowliness before men. O'Most Merciful of those who show mercy, You are the Lord of the weak and You are my Lord. To whom will You leave me? To a far-off stranger who will mistreat me? Or to an enemy to whom You have granted power over me? If You are not angry with me, then I care not, but Your favour is better for me. I seek refuge in the Light of Your Countenance by which the darkness is illumined and the things of this world and the next are set aright, lest Your anger descend upon me, or Your wrath light upon me. It is You Whom we beseech until You are well pleased. There is no power, and no strength except in You."

Please give this book a good review

Published for Allah (SWT), not for profit

100% the sale of this book provide food to those most in-need

www.ingramcontent.com/pod-product-compliance
Lightning Source LLC
Chambersburg PA
CBHW070334230426
43663CB00011B/2314